100+ Mixed Logic Puzzles
Word Search, Crossword, Kriss Kross,
Codeword, Sudoku and Maze
for Healthy Brain
with Bonus on The Last Page

CONTENTS

Instructions:

Crossword

You need to start solving with the longest word, they, as a rule, have a greater number of intersections with other words. If this is not the case, then choose the word that has the most intersections, even if it is not the largest. If you manage to guess this word, then its letters that are at the intersection with other words will be clues for solving them. Take on these words. The next stage of solving will lead to the fact that there will already be two or more clues for solving the words. Such words are, of course, easier to guess. In this way, move along the field and solve word by word.

Sudoku

• Only use each number once in each row, column, & grid.
• Avoid trying to guess the solution to the puzzle.
• Use the process of elimination as a tactic.
• Use cross-hatching and penciling in techniques.
• Only use the numbers 1 to 9.

Word Search

You will see a list of words on each page. The task is to find each word on the list and circle it. Words can be diagonal, backward, vertical and forward (downward or upward). Some words can be difficult to find so that it's better to use a pencil, in case you need to erase a mistake. Look at the example below of how each puzzle is presented.

Kriss Kross

To complete the puzzle you should place all the words inside the grid. This is only one way to fit all the words. If you fail, you can see the answers at the back.

Codeword

Codewords are crosswords without clues. Because of this, every letter of the alphabet has been replaced by a number, the same number representing the same letter throughout the puzzle. You have to decipher which letter matches which number. At the beginning, we show the codes for some of the letters. Enter these letters throughout the puzzle. It's necessary to start guessing words and opening new letters. If you get stuck, the answers you can see at the back of the book.

Tips and tricks for solving codewords:

• In most cases the highest number of the letters in the puzzle grid is a vowel.
• Look for letters of the alphabet that can appear as a double e.g. DD, EE, FF, GG
• Go through and cross of the letters A-Z and you will see what else you have to place.
• The letter S will often appear at the end of a word and act as a connecting letter for plural words.

Many words in the book are put together into one big word to complete the puzzle. These are words related to each other in a logical sequence, for example, you can meet: "XRAYSPEX"; which means: X-Ray Spex. As you can see, the word is spelled correctly due to the fact that it consists of several letters, we connect it to fill the puzzle completely.

You can always refer to the clues at the back of the book, and relying on your mind and logic, you can solve the puzzles, getting joy and benefit for your mind from the solutions of each of the puzzles.

Maze

The task in any of the labyrinths is to go from point A to point B. Enter and exit the labyrinth, that is, the main thing is to find a way out. You can try different paths, the main thing is to move evenly. It is forbidden to "jump" the walls and start solutions from a random point. The main thing is to go from beginning to end in one integral way.

1

Crossword

Across

5 Company that sponsors the Mariners' field (6)

7 Gawked (8)

9 Food suppliers (8)

10 Captain Marvel's magic word (6)

11 1960s sitcom set in a P.O.W. camp (12)

13 Basil and pine nut sauces (6)

15 High priest or priestess (6)

18 "Our Town" role (12)

21 Howard and Russell (6)

22 Places of instruction and learning (8)

23 Leading down the aisle (8)

24 Dishonored (6)

Down

1 Applicable (8)

2 Catnappers (6)

3 Sickening (8)

4 A lot of similar bodies, say? (6)

6 Scarf fabrics (8)

7 Adorned like beauty pageant contestants (6)

8 Like a friendly dog's tail (4)

12 Big things can be seen with it (8)

14 "___ Troopers" (Robert Heinlein book) (8)

16 Awed by (8)

17 Adjust a landscape (6)

18 One of the stuntmen on "Jackass" (6)

19 "Give me ___ or I quit!" (6)

20 Abs' neighbors (4)

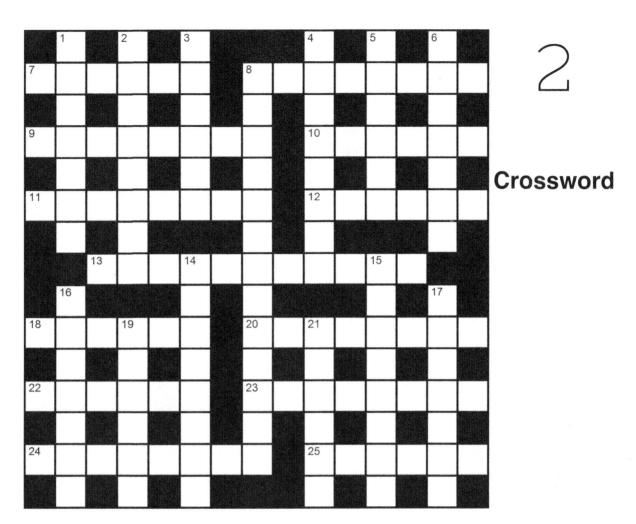

2 Crossword

Across

7 Indie rock star who composed the soundtrack to "Where the Wild Things Are" (2009) (6)

8 "Be right there!" (8)

9 Inconstant people (8)

10 Captain Marvel's transformation word (6)

11 "The Nation" writers, e.g. (8)

12 Big Dutch export (6)

13 STILLERS (11)

18 Causes strain (6)

20 Agree. (8)

22 Certain paddle-wielders (6)

23 Agoraphobe's anathema (8)

24 Hard (8)

25 95 things posted by Martin Luther (6)

Down

1 Babied, with "to" (7)

2 Drink causing forgetfulness of sorrow (8)

3 Bunnies or groupers (6)

4 Belie (8)

5 Aquatic nymphs of Greek myth (6)

6 Doe and hen (7)

8 1961 film based on "Romeo and Juliet" (13)

14 One charged (8)

15 It lets things go (8)

16 Bad-mouthed (7)

17 Any of 13 Catholic Church heads (7)

19 Encircled and attacked (6)

21 "Quinze" doubled (6)

Crossword

Across

7 Chewy candy (8)

9 Double platinum Genesis album of 1981 (6)

10 Groups of rels. (4)

11 Absolves (10)

12 "That sweet ___ of princes... ": Shak. (6)

14 Bearing tales. (8)

15 CarrySenecas (13)

17 Henri's oils (8)

19 "Oh man, that's bad" (6)

21 12/31 celebration site in Rio (10)

22 Amazes (4)

23 "Donna" singer (6)

24 The Atlantic's contents (8)

Down

1 Hymns of joy. (6)

2 Content sounds (4)

3 Drink of forgetfulness (8)

4 Best to follow, as advice (6)

5 Dessert made of eggs and sherry. (10)

6 Beauty contests (8)

8 Annie Oakley and others? (13)

13 Got rid of (10)

15 1982 media debut (8)

16 Deep-fried tortillas (8)

18 Not rife (6)

20 Apparently was (6)

22 "**yawn** I could use ___" (4)

4

Crossword

Across

8 Camp clothing label (8)

9 Become active (6)

10 "You think I won't try that?!" (6)

11 Details (8)

12 Crime-lab procedures (8)

13 A Cy Young Award winner: 1975 (6)

14 Item of apparel with spaghetti straps (15)

18 Carton-14 technicians (6)

20 Least adequate (8)

23 "Right this way" (8)

24 Old floorboard noise (6)

25 Hayes and Hunt (6)

26 Jiggled (8)

Down

1 Arthur's nephew (6)

2 Find a new home (8)

3 Brief appearances (6)

4 Comments from co-workers (15)

5 Looks convincingly like (8)

6 Bakery-cafe chain (6)

7 Bubbly beverages (8)

15 Bend forward (8)

16 How latitude lines run (8)

17 Came back (8)

19 "Dallas" matriarch and namesakes (6)

21 Brand from Holland (6)

22 Dividing elements (6)

5 Crossword

Across

1 Cool (13)

8 Bemires (with "down") (4)

9 *One blessed with ESP, perhaps (10)

10 "Heads up!" (6)

11 Easier to cut into (8)

12 Corral. (9)

14 (Puzzle by R. Santrey) Hoses down (4)

15 "... giving your heart to ___ to tear" (Kipling) (4)

16 Attentive escort. (9)

20 Practical jokers (8)

21 Drinks with straws (6)

23 *Apes whose habitat includes buckets and old bikes? (10)

24 Adieux, to Cato (4)

25 City driving hassles (13)

Down

1 Arrived furtively (7)

2 Baby ___ (daughter of "Dog the Bounty Hunter") (5)

3 Features of gymnasts' horses (7)

4 A century in American politics (15)

5 Bringing forth fruit, as corn (6)

6 Like some plugs (9)

7 Engine types (7)

13 "The Hunger Games" movie-franchise distributor (9)

15 Algonquian Indian (7)

17 "The ___" (1999 Pacino flick) (7)

18 Dieted (7)

19 1864 convention site (6)

22 "A penny saved is a penny earned," e.g. (5)

Crossword

6

Across

1 Manchester moms (6)

5 "To day shalt thou be with me in ___" (Lk 23:43) (8)

9 Fellow chairperson? (8)

10 End of a Seuss title (6)

11 Binoculars for the Met (12)

13 'hood (4)

14 Crooner (8)

17 Saviors (8)

18 Andover or Exeter: Abbr. (4)

20 Dairy Queen treat (12)

23 ( ), briefly (6)

24 Speculative (8)

25 Protective measures (8)

26 Daddy Warbucks employee (6)

Down

2 "... for the gain of ___": Swift (4)

3 Female hormones (9)

4 Joiner, of sorts (6)

5 Comments from co-workers (15)

6 Emitting percussive sounds (8)

7 "Fantasia" narrator Taylor (5)

8 "Lady and the Tramp" character (10)

12 Canines' favorite Timothy Bottoms film? (with "The") (10)

15 Groan elicitor (9)

16 Actions by some who woo (8)

19 Acknowledge, on the road (6)

21 "La vie ___" (high cost of living) (5)

22 "Betcha can't eat just one" potato chips (4)

7

Crossword

Across

7 Actor, usually (5)

8 Professional on a film set (9)

10 Facilitators (6)

11 Natural viewing height (8)

12 I'll have what he's having (8)

13 "Gotcha!" cries (4)

15 Actress Hudgens of "High School Musical" (7)

17 Co. with the longtime stock symbol "X" (7)

20 Content sounds (4)

22 Places for knots (8)

25 California island with a September wine fest (8)

26 Ancient Turkish landfall (6)

27 Loose cannons (9)

28 Abhorred (5)

Down

1 Headwear (9)

2 Visitors' announcement (8)

3 Cavorted. (7)

4 Circulation measure (8)

5 Bakery-cafe chain (6)

6 "I can ___ hint" (5)

9 "___ the pulse of summer in the ice" (Dylan Thomas) (4)

14 Whips up (9)

16 Place to order rolls (8)

18 Quickly detachable (8)

19 Like a boomerang (7)

21 Caesar's crown (6)

23 "Down with!" in Dijon (4)

24 Applied Rain-X to (5)

8

Crossword

Across

7 Courses for cars in competition (8)

9 Conquers, as a thirst (6)

10 About half of all elephants (4)

11 Visionary (10)

12 Anagram for senile (6)

14 Bigmouths (8)

15 He has a loop (6)

16 Catches sight of (6)

19 Journals (8)

21 "Say, boss, how about ___?" (6)

23 Ailment similar to spring fever (10)

24 Fashion model Wek (4)

25 Carpenter and Black (6)

26 Extra car keys, e.g. (8)

Down

1 Football fur: Var. (6)

2 Airport scanner units (4)

3 Setting for many pickups (8)

4 Adriatic peninsula shared by Italy, Slovenia and Croatia (6)

5 Renaissance composer (10)

6 Promise breakers (8)

8 Not rife (6)

13 Dieters' targets, say (10)

15 Shuttle locale for experiments (8)

17 Susan Lucci, for one (8)

18 "Given the circumstances... " (6)

20 Beat (6)

22 Big honey brand (6)

24 Amazes (4)

9

Crossword

Across

8 Believers in the spiritual unity of all people (6)

9 Four o'clock fare (8)

10 Security (8)

11 Put through a kitchen filter (6)

12 "Dramatis" follower (cast) (8)

13 "That's ___!" ("In all my years...") (6)

14 50 Cent or Dr. Dre (7)

17 Bridge contractor? (7)

20 "Blue-book" pieces (6)

22 Gave some help (8)

25 Computer command under "File" (6)

26 Interwove (8)

27 Ring leaders? (8)

28 Beats a rap, maybe (6)

Down

1 "Carmen" highlight (8)

2 "___ Lot" (King novel) (6)

3 "Your Best Life Now" author Joel (6)

4 Caches (7)

5 Little Rhody's neighbor (8)

6 Cosmetic fix (8)

7 Biblical outcasts (6)

15 "The Shawshank Redemption" setting (8)

16 Determines value (8)

18 Criticized severely (8)

19 "The Lord of the Rings" genre (7)

21 "The Secret ___" (1910 short story by Joseph Conrad) (6)

23 Accent: Mus. (6)

24 Hideous foe of Popeye (6)

Crossword

Across

8 City in central Kansas (6)

9 Cloisonne creator (8)

10 Like a straphanger (8)

11 ___ SHRDLU (6)

12 Carton-14 technicians (6)

13 Doors, at times (8)

15 Aimed ambitiously for, with "to" (7)

17 Blahs (7)

20 Spots for buckled babies (8)

22 Blew out (6)

23 Awards (6)

25 Fancy stands (8)

26 Angels' perches, around Christmastime (8)

27 Flew the coop, old-style (6)

Down

1 Drag venues (8)

2 Fortune-seeking trio (10)

3 Hindu garments (Var.) (6)

4 Dined. (7)

5 Neutral zone? (8)

6 "La Bamba" actress Elizabeth (4)

7 Camisole size (6)

14 Blue point, for one (10)

16 Home of Kendall College (8)

18 En brochette. (8)

19 Drag through the mud (7)

21 "Pied -___" (second home) (6)

22 Not thick (6)

24 "Am I invisible over here?" (4)

11

Crossword

Across

8 American quarters? (6)

9 Remove forcibly (8)

10 Beatle drummer before Ringo (8)

11 Elon Musk company (6)

12 Latin (6)

13 Cliff-hanger? (8)

14 "Decisions, decisions..." (7)

16 Colorful violets (7)

20 Reason for getting in at dawn, say (8)

23 40 winks (6)

25 European silver coins of old (6)

26 Turquoise in Arizona and New Mexico (8)

27 It can't pick up many distant objects (8)

28 Embarrassed (6)

Down

1 Form a political union (8)

2 Coeur ___ (6)

3 One in taxing circumstances (8)

4 Believer in a strong centralized government (7)

5 Dos follow (6)

6 Chewy candy (8)

7 Assessors (6)

15 Impaled (8)

17 Sirrah, for example. (8)

18 Covered, as cookware (8)

19 1992 N.H.L. M.V.P. (7)

21 Town across the Connecticut River from Springfield, Mass. (6)

22 Brand from Holland (6)

24 It may be picked up at Vesuvio (6)

Crossword

Across

8 Reduce to tears? (8)

9 Have a ___ the table (6)

10 Body of water between France and Switzerland (10)

11 "Anna and the King of ___" (4)

12 "Nick of Time" actress Mason (6)

14 Reason to use a room freshener (8)

15 Endowed with land (7)

17 Able to see in the dark (7)

20 First son, sometimes (8)

22 "Two Mules for ___ Sara" (6)

24 "Last Jedi" general (4)

25 "Le Morte d'Arthur" figure (10)

27 "Frank Sinatra Has a Cold" author Gay (6)

28 Sweat, so to speak (8)

Down

1 "Hakuna ___" (6)

2 1970s astronaut Slayton (4)

3 Camp clothing label (8)

4 Game in which captured pieces are turned upside down (7)

5 Albeniz composition "Cantos de ___" (6)

6 "Moon Shadow" singer (10)

7 Beat decisively (8)

13 Flaky person (10)

16 Geography illustration. (8)

18 Palliated (8)

19 Anticipating a decline (7)

21 "Jeopardy!" question (6)

23 Internet hookups? (6)

26 "127 Hours" subject Ralston (4)

13

Crossword

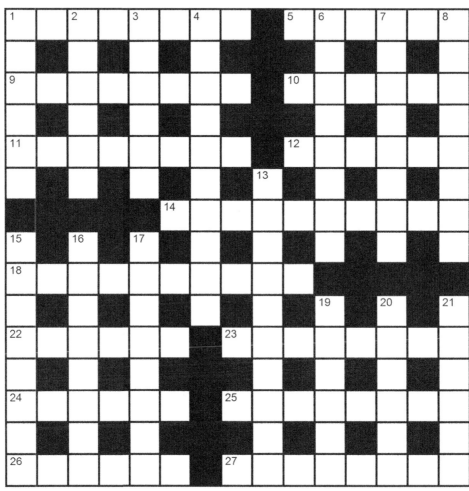

Across

1 *Space traveler (8)

5 People down under? (6)

9 Communication carriers (8)

10 "Macbeth" witch (6)

11 Canal zone entrances? (8)

12 "Appasionata," for one (6)

14 Acted out publicly (10)

18 Spot designers (10)

22 Beatty role (6)

23 Gilda Radner character on "SNL" (8)

24 Mitigates (6)

25 Beget (8)

26 Mount St. Helens, e.g. (6)

27 Campers' carry-alongs (8)

Down

1 Did in (6)

2 "Terms of Endearment" heroine (6)

3 Creature with a paddlelike tail (6)

4 Lack of gracefulness. (10)

6 Bar of a sort (8)

7 Issues forth (8)

8 Moved up and down. (8)

13 African native (10)

15 Looks convincingly like (8)

16 Event with cakes and cookies (8)

17 Visitors' first words (8)

19 Cry from comic book civilians (6)

20 "Green Hills of Africa" journey (6)

21 Hay gatherers (6)

Crossword 14

Across

1 Gift for a music lover. (12)

10 "Whenever, Wherever" singer (7)

11 Tentacled gastropod (7)

12 "Smart" guys (5)

13 "The March of Time" production (8)

15 Sorority (10)

16 Big ref. books (4)

18 "High" bodies (4)

20 Be good (10)

22 Came forth (from) (8)

24 A short pass play (5)

26 New York City bridge, informally, with "the" (7)

27 Crystalline mineral (7)

28 Motion picture industry (12)

Down

2 Active participants (7)

3 Certain publications. (8)

4 "Come to the Mardi ___" (song) (4)

5 Common come-on (10)

6 Cabbage dishes. (5)

7 Cat with colorful points (7)

8 1995 Kevin Spacey movie (with "The") (13)

9 Library specialty. (13)

14 Baldy (10)

17 Independent counsel during the Bill Clinton scandal (8)

19 Slow dances, in ballet (7)

21 "How about that" (7)

23 Agitated, poetically (5)

25 "She dwell among the untrodden ___": Wordsworth (4)

15

Crossword

Across

1 Cleaned up and ready to go (13)

10 "... ___ with Nineveh and Tyre." (5)

11 Naomi Campbell, e.g. (9)

12 Service charges (9)

13 A layoff, unpolitely (5)

14 Action after a yellow flag (7)

16 "Insecure" actress (7)

18 Blotter entries. (7)

20 "The Player" star (7)

22 Adhan orators (5)

24 Brother of Menelaus (9)

26 Be a perfect example (9)

27 "___ of information." (5)

28 Children's author Helen ___ (13)

Down

2 High-up workers (7)

3 Really reels (9)

4 Alan-___ of ballads (5)

5 Certain word puzzles (9)

6 Anticipate eagerly. (5)

7 Boots, gloves, mask, etc. (7)

8 Group dealing with hard stuff? (13)

9 GREEN (13)

15 Conductor of opera rising in encore (9) (9)

17 Garage find (9)

19 Apprehend clearly. (7)

21 "... but we must cultivate our garden" (7)

23 "To Kill a Mockingbird" character (5)

25 "... beneath ___ blue sky": Don Henley lyric (5)

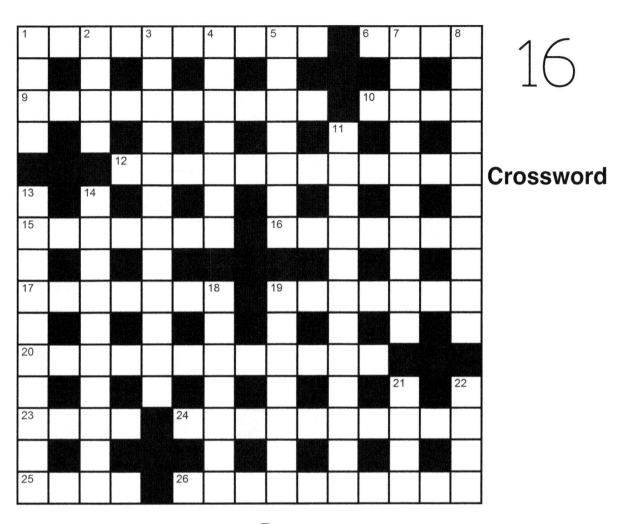

16

Crossword

Across

1 All-year voucher (10)

6 "Opal" or "coal" ending (4)

9 Financially viable (10)

10 2016 NBA champs (4)

12 "Looking back..." (12)

15 Humiliators (7)

16 More Broadway-bound? (7)

17 "Here and there is born a Saint ___, foundress of nothing... ": "Middlemarch" (7)

19 French "sainte" (7)

20 "David" creator (12)

23 "Representing Music" org. (4)

24 Acquiesce (10)

25 Acted like (4)

26 Composition of a proverbial soft bed (10)

Down

1 Barcelona Mmes. (4)

2 10-stringed lute (4)

3 2001 George Clooney movie (12)

4 "Ave Maria" and "Kaddish," e.g. (7)

5 GMC trucks (7)

7 It runs through southern Idaho (10)

8 Con artist's ideal victim (10)

11 Waiver words? (12)

13 Columbus : ___ ::... (10)

14 Effort toward a law degree (10)

18 24 hours back (7)

19 Checkout offering (7)

21 "___ Nagila" (4)

22 Astronaut William of Apollo 8 (4)

17

Crossword

Across

1 Fountain employe: Slang. (8)

5 Coeur ___, Idaho (6)

10 Cottage style (7)

11 "Yo Mama" jokes, e.g. (7)

12 A forum is for 'em (5)

13 Established ownership, as of land (9)

14 Fulfillment... and #2 on the list (12)

18 "7 Rings" singer (January, 2019) (12)

21 Builds oneself up (9)

23 "Toora ___..." (Irish lullaby syllables) (5)

24 Facile quality (7)

25 Cat. (7)

26 Banzai Pipeline user (6)

27 Mimics convincingly (8)

Down

1 "___ me!" (6)

2 Abaxial (6)

3 He was Sonny to Marlon Brando's Vito (9)

4 Action that can lead to feeling bushed? (14)

6 "Happy Days" actor Williams (5)

7 Quirkily varied (8)

8 Legal right of way (8)

9 Antacid name since 1872 (14)

15 Eldorados, e.g. (9)

16 3/17 musicmaker (8)

17 7,926 miles, for Earth (8)

19 Basic beach gear (6)

20 Cavalry issues (6)

22 "Dog Day Afternoon" event (5)

18

Crossword

Across

1 Go after, like with a housefly (6)

4 Counting devices. (8)

9 Inscribed monuments (6)

10 *Oil, jocularly (8)

12 ""L'___, c'est moi"" (4)

13 "Rules of Engagement" actor (10)

15 Make tracks (12)

18 It spins its reels (12)

21 Circus team (10)

22 "... is ___ itself": F.D.R. (4)

24 Boards Amtrak (8)

25 Asiatic princesses (6)

26 !, to a printer (8)

27 Determine how much damage was done, e.g. (6)

Down

1 Fiction genre (8)

2 "I say unto you" preceder (8)

3 "Take down ___ or two" (4)

5 Condition of a Ute's coif? (12)

6 Certain contemporary collegians (10)

7 Avoid making changes (6)

8 Joint maker. (6)

11 Geology, e.g. (12)

14 "The Liberation of L. B. Jones" actress (10)

16 Me-tooism phrase (8)

17 Anxiety may be a symptom of it (8)

19 Draws toward evening (6)

20 "Friends, Romans, countrymen..." sort of speaker (6)

23 Waters, informally (4)

Sudoku

1

6	2			9				4
					8			
		8		6				
	9	1		4		2		
		3				1		
4	8	5						6
	1	4						2
7			4					
			1	9				

2

		9			6			4
		6	4	3			9	
	7					5		
	5		8	9			7	1
	8			5	9			6
			2					8
		1	7				2	
4				8				

3

4						1	3	
	8						5	7
		6	5					
			3	9				
	2		4		6			
			8				4	
	7			6	9	4		
	5			7		6		
1								

4

2		1						
	5	2						
			1			8		
	7					6		
			6					4
5	3	9						
	4				6	7		
					7	4		1
8	6				3			9

Sudoku

5

3			9			5	7	
9			2				4	
2	8						1	
			3			6		7
				5			3	
				7				
7				1				
	6			9				
	5		7	3			8	

6

8			3				6	
		1	5					9
			2					
	3				7			
	8	9	6				4	
1	4						3	
7					5	9		
	2					5		7
		6				1		

7

	1			9			3	6
			4		8			
	2	8		7				
	6				4			7
					3			4
			8			1		
3			7	1				
	8	4	3			5		6

8

					3		6	
		2	5			4		3
4				9		2		
9		1				5		
		4				9		
					6		7	5
							9	1
			7					4
8				3	1			

Sudoku

9

9		5	1				2	3
1			6	5				
5				4		8		9
	7					1		
8							5	7
	8				4			2
				7		3		
2					1	5		

10

3		9		1				
			2		7			
		8			6	5		
	7	6	3		1			
				9		4		
			7		5			2
	6				9	3	8	
		1		6				
						9		

11

		4	8			2	1	
			3		6			
9		1						
5				4				7
1	2	6						
		8	9					
				5	4			
	1		4			6		
6		7		8				9

12

	8		4			5	7	2
				1		9		
	9					6		
		9	5					1
	2							
	7	3		9	4	6		
6		2					3	
	3						5	
						2		8

Sudoku

13

			7			5	3	
3	6		4					
					8	9		
5							9	
8			3	4				
1	7			9				5
		1						
		4			6	7		
			8		3	6	2	

14

	3						7	
8			4		6		3	5
3							1	9
1	2			7	8			
	6		1			7		
	4		6	9	3			
	9					2		
7						5		

15

		8			7	9		
	7							6
			1	4	6			
				8		5		2
	5		6					
2			9	3				1
				2	9			
	3	6					5	
		9				4	7	

16

		5				2		
6			2				9	
			9			8		7
8			1					3
	4	6	8					
	9			7		6		
2						1		
3		7						
9	8						7	4

Sudoku

17

		6	2		1			
4	3							
8				9	3			
	6					8		7
		5						
	1			7			2	
			1	5	6			
		7			3			5
	9			3		4		

18

	3	9	5	7				
					2			7
	2		3		9			5
				8	1			
3	6		7					
	4	7		3				
			8	9				6
		1					8	
								3

Word Search № 1

```
E M A N C I P A T I O N O N F W A
N S P R O S C E N I U M R D E
E E O M I D W I V E S N N Z T
V X I T H K V R O Y Y A J C R
G T R T E U O L X S G E C I E
V E R S R R K R X U E A V N M
S N P I Y A I C T V R E C E O
P D G E G X N C B Y D M D M L
H E R W I L F Q K I U A Z A O
A D A E N U R R U H W G G A H
R I N M D M E T M I F E N C S
A P D N J K N X P U L A T T S
O Z E E X Z Z M R X Y I O A L
H H U Y E Q Y V A S W N T F A
H O R R I B L E F S K N U Y G
```

TREMOLO	MIDWIVES	KNOTS
SWITCH	PROSCENIUM	SEED
PHARAOH	EXTENDED	CINEMA
KERKYRA	EMANCIPATION	SLAG (Ferra)
YANA	ESOTERIC	UGANDA
FRENZY	GRANDEUR	AXLE
TRANQUILITY	HORRIBLE	

Word Search № 2

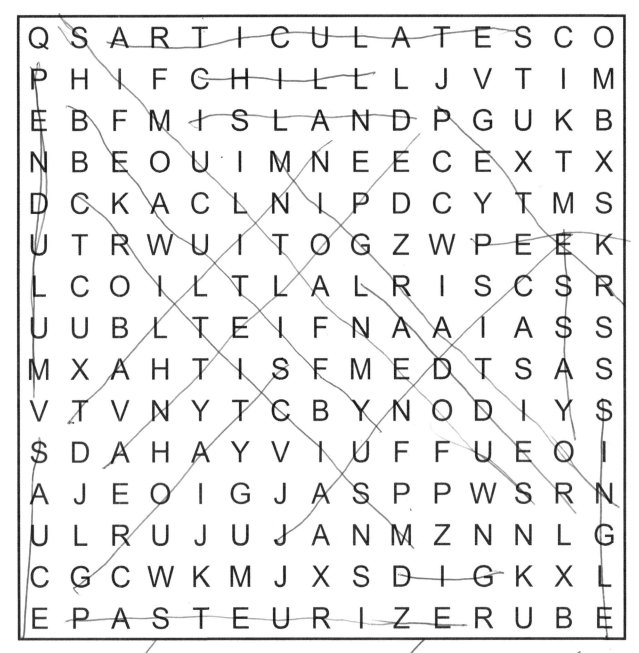

```
Q S A R T I C U L A T E S C O
P H I F C H I L L L J V T I M
E B F M I S L A N D P G U K B
N B E O U I M N E E C E X T X
D C K A C L N I P D C Y T M S
U T R W U I T O G Z W P E E K
L C O I L T L A L R I S C S R
U U B L T E I F N A A I A S S
M X A H T I S F M E D T S A S
V T V N Y T C B Y N O D I Y S
S D A H A Y V I U F F U E O I
A J E O I G J A S P P W S R N
U L R U J U J A N M Z N N L G
C G C W K M J X S D I G K X L
E P A S T E U R I Z E R U B E
```

CHILL ✓	PENDULUM ✓	SINGLE ✓
GROATS ✓	DIG ✓	ANTELOPE ✓
TALLINN ✓	ARTICULATE ✓	CRITICISM ✓
PETER ✓	MIGRATION ✓	BEAUTIFY ✓
PEEK ✓	SIMULTANEOUS ✓	PASTEURIZE ✓
JAUNDICE ✓	ISLAND ✓	LADDER ✓
ESSAY ✓	SAUCE ✓	

Word Search № 3

C	G	S	P	L	E	A	S	I	N	G	W	E	Y	F
L	G	C	J	S	L	I	D	O	H	A	Q	V	S	L
C	E	R	A	M	I	C	S	H	S	W	Z	H	L	L
J	V	I	R	T	Z	Z	T	R	P	X	S	U	Y	V
T	E	M	F	Y	U	Y	A	A	O	U	B	R	K	V
A	R	S	M	H	M	C	T	W	B	W	O	X	N	C
C	G	H	Q	V	Z	S	I	Q	J	T	A	A	C	S
N	L	A	O	S	A	F	Y	D	C	P	M	N	O	M
A	A	W	I	L	O	L	V	I	O	Y	T	V	M	S
V	D	Z	T	E	G	M	V	Q	E	R	R	T	P	A
B	E	U	E	S	W	Y	B	G	C	A	A	E	U	N
A	O	T	O	K	W	A	O	R	M	M	C	E	T	J
R	E	A	T	Q	R	B	O	E	E	I	T	R	E	V
W	H	I	N	T	O	N	E	G	B	D	R	H	S	E
C	S	T	O	C	H	A	S	T	I	C	L	D	C	S

ROWAN ✓   INTONE ✓   BICEPS ✓

DOHA ✓   COMPUTE ✓   CHAOS ✓

TRACT ✓   OUTLAST ✓   STOCHASTIC ✓

EVERGLADE ✓   BULL ✓   BOGEYMAN ✓

PYRAMID ✓   PLEASING ✓   CERAMICS ✓

MYTH ✓   SOMBRE ✓   VICTORY ✓

SCRIMSHAW ✓   BUSH ✓

Word Search № 4

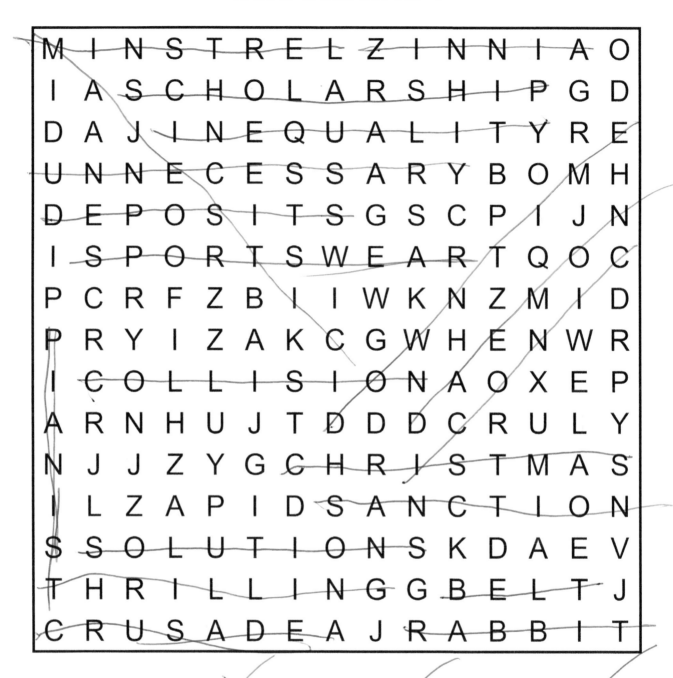

M I N S T R E L Z I N N I A O
I A S C H O L A R S H I P G D
D A J I N E Q U A L I T Y R E
U N N E C E S S A R Y B O M H
D E P O S I T S G S C P I J N
I S P O R T S W E A R T Q O C
P C R F Z B I I W K N Z M I D
P R Y I Z A K C G W H E N W R
I C O L L I S I O N A O X E P
A R N H U J T D D D C R U L Y
N J J Z Y G C H R I S T M A S
I L Z A P I D S A N C T I O N
S S O L U T I O N S K D A E V
T H R I L L I N G G B E L T J
C R U S A D E A J R A B B I T

UNNECESSARY   CHRISTMAS   MINSTREL
ZINNIA   RABBIT   BELT
ICONIC   SCHOLARSHIP SANCTION
DAEMON   DEPOSITS   INEQUALITY
MAJESTIC   COLLISION   SOLUTIONS
DOWNTIME   CRUSADE   SPORTSWEAR
PIANIST   THRILLING

Word Search № 5

```
S G E O R G E T T E P F A S Q
H U B M M A G A Z I N E S N G
E R Z U U H P S D O O C T N J
N H V N W C U F K Z I M I K S
Z O R D B K U U I R P G Y M L
H L J J R C S N T S G R E O C
E L H A O P H C H O C L O M G
N Y B M T C E I L A B A D A H
G W R E H L L B C O P J L R E
L O S N E K E W R K I P Q S I
O O O A R P H P Y D C L Y U R
E D E X S A S Y S I R A I P E
S T R A N S M I S S I O N I S
S P H O T O G R A P H S W A S
I N H I B I T O R U D D R L G
```

MAGAZINES	HEIRESS	INHIBITOR
SHENZHEN	PHOTOGRAPHS	PROBLEMS
BLOGGING	MARSUPIAL	ELECTRIC
SUKON	FISCAL	UNHAPPY
LOESS	CHICK	NDJAMENA
SIRAI	BROTHERS	HOLLYWOOD
TRANSMISSION	GEORGETTE	

31

Word Search № 6

```
H Y P O T H E S I S J G M J G
W E S C O F U V U B N G P B P
F L T O B E K V E I N S D P H
W T R N T W N N K I M C F M Y
A L E T C O I O T M A D Y L S
T I P R Q H R H A O X F D D I
T C I I S T C D H R I T E E C
E E D B S A R G G L L Q M P I
N N A U Y S H O V E L S C R A
T S T T A O K A P I A F U E N
I I I I N I K O L A E V B S Q
O N O O P T I C I A N E S S H
N G N N R E F E R R A L S I J
A S H L O R G A N I Z E X O B
D I L E T T A N T E B R Y N X
```

PHYSICIAN	CUBS	HYPOTHESIS
REFERRALS	NIKOLAEV	STROKING
MAXILLA	DILETTANTE	SHOVELS
TREPIDATION	OPTICIAN	RITE
ORGANIZE	LICENSING	APIA
ATTENTION	DEPRESSION	CONTRIBUTION
YACHTING	SHINE	

32

Word Search № 7

```
Q C D D C T W H I T N E Y D V
U A E I X R M Z H C V O V I U
A T B A V E B O Y I K P O C R
D A A L N L A E T F H T Q T U
R F U O K A G E L U S C S A I
I A C G M X R I I F R X A T N
L L H U I C X N U J A J M E O
A Q E E E C A K S U R S D K N
T U R S L H E V O N N T T B C
E E Y K C E W E F T L E E C H
R X Y A N M S A R A G R A R A
A U H P C I U S E E J M Y Q L
L C P A R S I M O N I O U S A
P E A C E E E G A N A C H E N
B E S P R I T V B P R J U G T
```

JUNTA	DICTATE	GANACHE
SECRETIVE	BELFAST	CHACHANI
QUADRILATERAL	PEACE	LEECH
RELAX	ESPRIT	DIALOGUE
PARSIMONIOUS	DEBAUCHERY	SARAGRAR
NONCHALANT	LESSON	WHITNEY
CHEMISE	CATAFALQUE	

33

Word Search № 8

```
D U P R Y P S D J C I M J U V
M I T T E N S S T A R A E N Z
S N V J X I A U S E L N M L W
G I T O D F O S W O F D R E V
O N R N H Y A O N B S M I A X
H N O G A K L A E I I S P S E
V I U L L F R D O U B T S H X
I N G E N G A G I T A T I O N
G G H U E D P Y I N P I B T J
O S S R P R O C E D U R E S M
R H I S T O R I C A L M G Q S
P A C I F I S T K F A Q C F L
X O E U R A S I A S S U I R E
X N Y K Q H C Q G D M D O V E
P F A D P M Y U O E R J G N P
```

SUNFLOWER   GRANOLA   SAMET

MITTENS   LAYOUT   JONGLEUR

HISTORICAL   PACIFIST   INNINGS

EURASIA   AMEX   SLEEP

VIGOR   AGITATION   DOUBTS

PROCEDURES   TROUGH   KASSAI

UNLEASH   MANDMS

34

Word Search № 9

```
F N O N A L C O H O L I C K Q
O A D E C O M P O S E D K N S
L N I N E F F E C T U A L L Y
K N O O F G G R E E N L A N D
L U C A N I A E V S P Q N O G
O L O M U R S I I N N O G N E
R M D Z V E A T I Z I R I K T
E E Z Y R W I R B T E R N H T
N N A O M R T Z A D E N K R Y
S T F J T S C T N E I R O N S
A B U N A N N U N B Q Q Z X B
I F A G D E M I T A S S E Y U
Z K Z C M Z G S D V M I A D R
M I G A O N H M E M B E R S G
M N L F E P V P I R A T E T F
```

LAMENTATION	IRONS	ENGINEERING
GETTYSBURG	GREENLAND	MEMBERS
ANTRITIS	LUCANIA	PIRATE
DEMITASSE	FORESEE	NONALCOHOLIC
ANNULMENT	WAIVE	UNDERGO
FOLKLORE	DECOMPOSED	GASTRIN
ABUNA	INEFFECTUALLY	

Word Search № 10

```
P R O V I D E R B A N E P V B
C R E F L I D K C S O D R T U
O A P P G S J A P N T L E N L
N S I Y R T N C C N C D C A L
M T T E A R P U L P I T A P E
K O O H A U M W T L P U R P T
A U M L J S A N A Q S H I R P
R N E O S T E V C L P T O A R
L D L N V R N J S U K J U I O
U X A O E I B R R I M E S S O
K E D F P R E S I D U E R E F
J M F U R F W U T Z H A A S M
R I T P E K I P U W W I P Z A
D Y L Y T B F H A G A P Z X B
M V V I Q T E L L E R Z P I V
```

ASTOUND	PRET	WALKERS
RESIDUE	KARLUK	BULLETPROOF
DIFFERENT	WIFE	PULPIT
PROVIDER	RITUAL	CUM
INVALID	LARNACA	DISTRUST
PRECARIOUS	EPITOME	APPRAISE
JEANS	TELLER	

Word Search № 11

```
S F O R T U I T O U S Y K T X
H D U C K L I N G L H E N T L
O R O O M M A T E P G E P A F
R I M K O W J J A D D J T M W
T F I T K T I R I N C I T K D
C B L O Q Q G R U B G Y J F T
U C I P H O T M E I V S Z V D
T O T M I R G V D S O M U S G
S N A B A I P F S T A F F T S
A J N P S J K M D Z U E W A W
T U T U Q V D C E V F Y F I E
C R E A T I O N N T R E U N E
Y E J D O M I N I C A D V E K
A S P I C E X V M W Y J X D O
E C O M P A T I B I L I T Y A
```

WIRES	COMPATIBILITY	BIOGRAPHY
SPICE	PARTRIDGE	EYED
SHORTCUTS	GMUNDEN	DIGITAL
STAFF	FORTUITOUS	DUCKLING
WEEK	DENIM	CONJURES
ROOMMATE	STAINED	DOMINICA
MILITANT	CREATION	

Word Search № 12

```
C O N T R O V E R S Y P L A U
V N W E P S U B S I D Y L N M
I B E W G B G R E A T E R T G
G O K S K O P E L O S L M L M
N R V A T Z D E R Y A M W E E
E D D I H E G P H T I D M R T
T E R K L E A C N T D I A S H
T N S T L K R E I O Y O Y V A
E N T L W A N V X E L D F S N
O O O W G I S W D L O L T E
M C E I T J T P D Y I M Y O L
B R L N U A K C D Q C O R R U
U O O V Z M C O H L R L B M A
Q C O R R E C T I O N A B S O
G R A V E Y A R D K G E F T R
```

METHANE   VIGNETTE   SKOPELOS

GAB   TWITCH   STORMS

MAYFLY   VITIM   CONTINENTAL

GREATER   ANTLERS   CORRECTION

MOTTLED   BORDEN   OLIGARCHY

SUBSIDY   GRAVEYARD   CONTROVERSY

IDYLLIC   COLLEGE

38

Word Search № 13

```
G F O R A Y Q C R W A W D K D
S E N B X T W M Y R I A D Y I
Z Q O U R A C C E P T I N G S
B C W R M E Q S Y X Y Q Q O S
E H X D G E E C H O P P E D O
S A M V F E R Z Q W X G Q N L
P N V O K B S I E T N Z Z A V
U D S F C E G Z C K P G Y G E
R S H A H C D W G A T P B E Y
T Y C C N I C E G P L T W J M
Q C T Z Z T Y N L I U E B E G
O A T I E D O Z E K S J U C D
W T A N G E R I N E C H E T I
H H J F C O A G U L A T E T N
O P A L E S C E N T U Q I L A
```

FORAY	TIED	CHOPPED
MYRIAD	BREEZE	NUMERICAL
WATCHES	OPALESCENT	EJECT
SPURT	DINA	DISSOLVE
TANGERINE	GEORGE	NICE
SANTO	HANDS	ACCEPTING
GLEN	COAGULATE	

Word Search № 14

```
B O O K M A K E R L C B L T J
E S Y A S L Y T A D Q A T M C
C E C H M T P E Q V I R Y Y R
A U J W O D R R T C M B J W Y
V A A K F O V A I A I E L C S
I K L G B R B F I O N R G B T
T R B V F I E N Q U B A T A
I H A C G T L L T V E C F R L
E K N B R I S A Z E T M F E N
S I I A U E K B O D A A G N E
A S A Q N A Q U S Q L R P D X
X S A S P P O R O S U K R S P
D E M E T E R N F P X S D X I
Y S B X T B A U I N E R F Q R
R O A M I N G M H K U U M B E
```

KISSES

GAFF

DEMETER

MARKS

MINUET

LABURNUM

ALBANIA

BOOKMAKER

PURGE

ROAMING

ALTDORF

CRYSTAL

EXPIRE

AQUILEIA

POROS

ARTIFICIAL

ARBOREAL

CAVITIES

BARBER

TRENDS

Word Search № 15

```
N V E N T I F A C T J B L Y H
C O V E R C O M E C W A S X N
C R T F E A R S O M E A M O P
H E M I S P H E R E B E I E B
D P C W A A L B O R G T A E S
B S T E E P S V E X S O D U M
A P S W N O Z C T E E A T Y B
R E X Y L J N Y G L H N R B E
I K U B P A L G B S A U J U X
S K Y U R F U B C N N B E R P
T B Y U I S U M G E X D X N R
A S D F C R O U P N F T T I E
A N Q F E N P Y A H H B Q S S
E S S E Y E X I Q O W Q Q H S
Q W L T R I C K S T E R S E N
```

STEEP	PENURY	SUGGESTION
VENTIFACT	OVERCOME	PRICEY
EXPRESS	JAMES	TRICKSTERS
AALBORG	BARISTA	REPUGNANT
NOT	BURNISH	FEARSOME
HEMISPHERE	ENDURANCE	BYBLOS
SHADE	RUBBLE	

Word Search № 16

```
N S K S C H O L A R S H I P S
I T Y E V E N T S C O T T A G
F U R E P R E S E N T N Y T Z
A F K B J P W A G N E R I A N
C F Z N L U F D O Z A W U S S
U E M H Z I L R I S E L L N I
L R O E P E P H E A S A N T G
T K W O I P G N A W B Z N Q H
Y R F F N P I U P M Z N A T T
J C R V Q P Z A I A C O S T S
N I H C S Z Y G Z L F B A R H
A D X P F Z A W Q W T U J G X
P H O S P H A T E X K Y U I O
I T L E C O N S U M P T I O N
C L E R O I D E A H O W N B M
```

TOPSPIN	COSTS	FACULTY
KOHL	RISE	PHEASANT
PHOSPHATE	COTTA	WAGNERIAN
CONSUMPTION	GUILTY	BUY
AIRFIELD	STUFFER	SIGHTS
CLEROIDEA	GIMBALS	EVENTS
SCHOLARSHIPS	REPRESENT	

Word Search № 17

```
T W R E G I S T R A T I O N X
H V D O M I N A T E E E O Y V
D I E S T A N D O U T I T F O
S B T R F B N A T I O N S U L
Y B D O B Y H H I U B C S K E
B R E A K A W A Y M N W Z A R
T Y X P H R L T M O M E N T F
S M I R A G E L C Z V N S Z B
O L G K C K C S Y P O L L O I
Z R E M E M B E R I N G C X R
O H O R R I F I C F P Y T V D
P N E U M O C O N I O S I S Q
O B D S E E D L I N G S N G F
L E A F H O P P E R S I I T H
S A L V A T O R E P K Z C L E
```

BIRD	TUNES	OLE
HORRIFIC	SOZOPOL	STANDOUT
SEEDLINGS	VERBALLY	REMEMBERING
NATIONS	BREAKAWAY	REGISTRATION
DOMINATE	POLLO	SIDE
LEAFHOPPERS	SALVATORE	MOMENT
PNEUMOCONIOSIS	MIRAGE	

Word Search № 18

```
D E L I C A T E S S E N G P J
P E P P E R S D C Y F O R T Y
C M S S X S A Y O K F X D T D
L Z B V Y R I W T C N H V A S
A J E P T O S U I O M U Q P W
N H D N P A O J L U A G U S K
D R R D R B M Q L N C P G C T
E X O U E S E M I T P Z A A G
S O O Y S U T R O E A Z L R M
T F M E E R R A N R N Q H V T
I K B U N D Y B C F T C S E B
N W W L T S V B Z E H Z T S O
E C R Y S T A L S I E C A E V
M A P H R A O E D T R I B H U
Y M F X E R Q U E E N S S P O
```

STAR   COTILLION   PRESENTS

COUNTERFEIT   PANTHER   DELICATESSEN

FORTY   APART   FOUR

BEDROOM   STAB   CRYSTALS

ABSURD   MAPHRAO   PEPPERS

RABBLE   SCARVES   QUEENS§§

CLANDESTINE   ISOMETRY

44

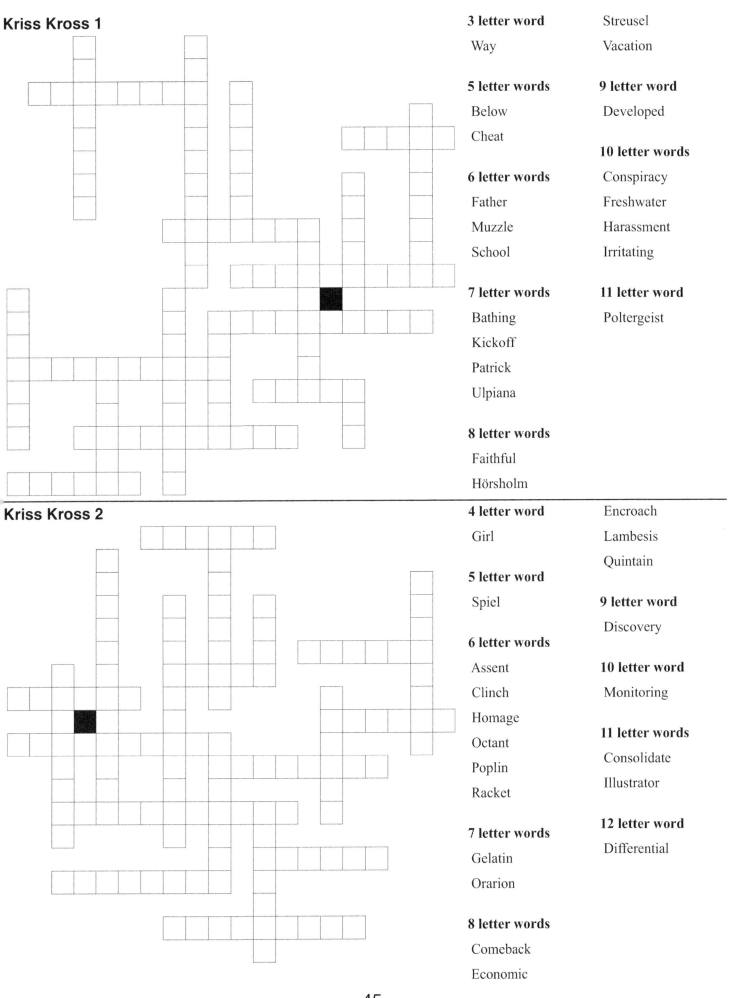

Kriss Kross 1

3 letter word
Way

5 letter words
Below
Cheat

6 letter words
Father
Muzzle
School

7 letter words
Bathing
Kickoff
Patrick
Ulpiana

8 letter words
Faithful
Hörsholm

Streusel
Vacation

9 letter word
Developed

10 letter words
Conspiracy
Freshwater
Harassment
Irritating

11 letter word
Poltergeist

Kriss Kross 2

4 letter word
Girl

5 letter word
Spiel

6 letter words
Assent
Clinch
Homage
Octant
Poplin
Racket

7 letter words
Gelatin
Orarion

8 letter words
Comeback
Economic

Encroach
Lambesis
Quintain

9 letter word
Discovery

10 letter word
Monitoring

11 letter words
Consolidate
Illustrator

12 letter word
Differential

Kriss Kross 3

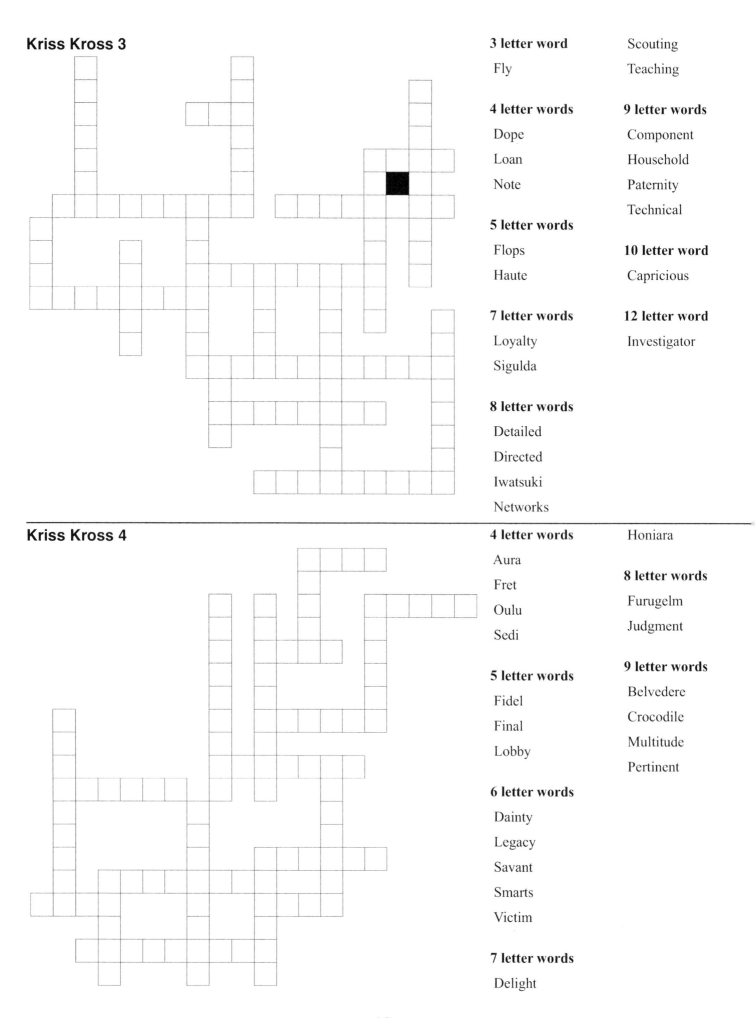

3 letter word
Fly

4 letter words
Dope
Loan
Note

5 letter words
Flops
Haute

7 letter words
Loyalty
Sigulda

8 letter words
Detailed
Directed
Iwatsuki
Networks

Scouting
Teaching

9 letter words
Component
Household
Paternity
Technical

10 letter word
Capricious

12 letter word
Investigator

Kriss Kross 4

4 letter words
Aura
Fret
Oulu
Sedi

5 letter words
Fidel
Final
Lobby

6 letter words
Dainty
Legacy
Savant
Smarts
Victim

7 letter words
Delight

Honiara

8 letter words
Furugelm
Judgment

9 letter words
Belvedere
Crocodile
Multitude
Pertinent

Kriss Kross 5

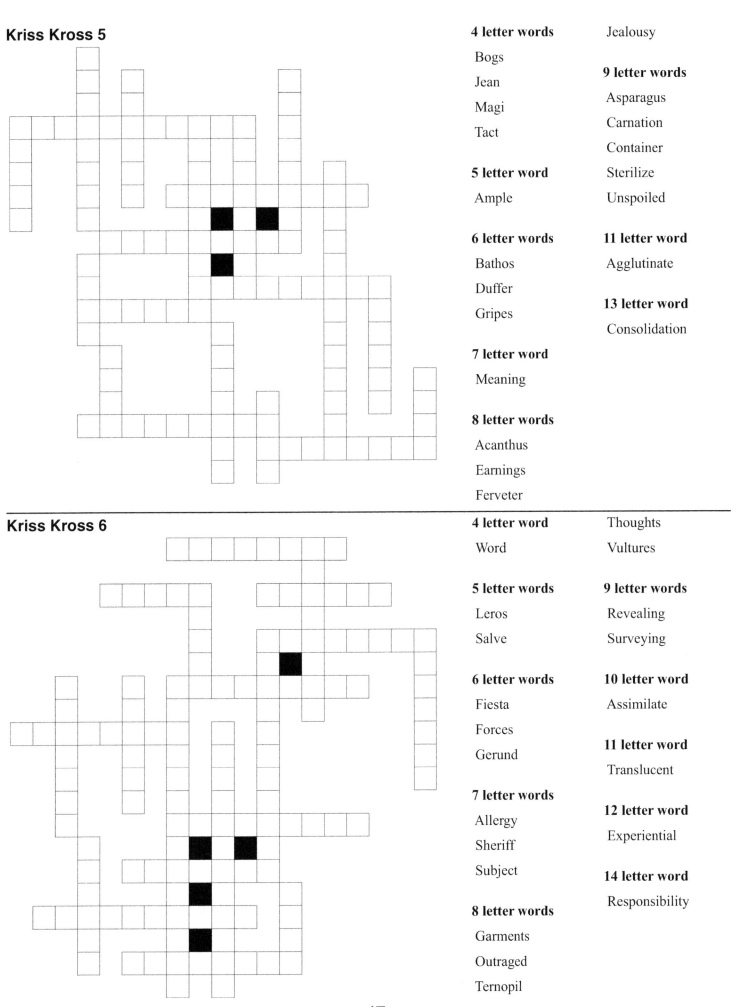

4 letter words
Bogs
Jean
Magi
Tact

5 letter word
Ample

6 letter words
Bathos
Duffer
Gripes

7 letter word
Meaning

8 letter words
Acanthus
Earnings
Ferveter

Jealousy

9 letter words
Asparagus
Carnation
Container
Sterilize
Unspoiled

11 letter word
Agglutinate

13 letter word
Consolidation

Kriss Kross 6

4 letter word
Word

5 letter words
Leros
Salve

6 letter words
Fiesta
Forces
Gerund

7 letter words
Allergy
Sheriff
Subject

8 letter words
Garments
Outraged
Ternopil

Thoughts
Vultures

9 letter words
Revealing
Surveying

10 letter word
Assimilate

11 letter word
Translucent

12 letter word
Experiential

14 letter word
Responsibility

Kriss Kross 7

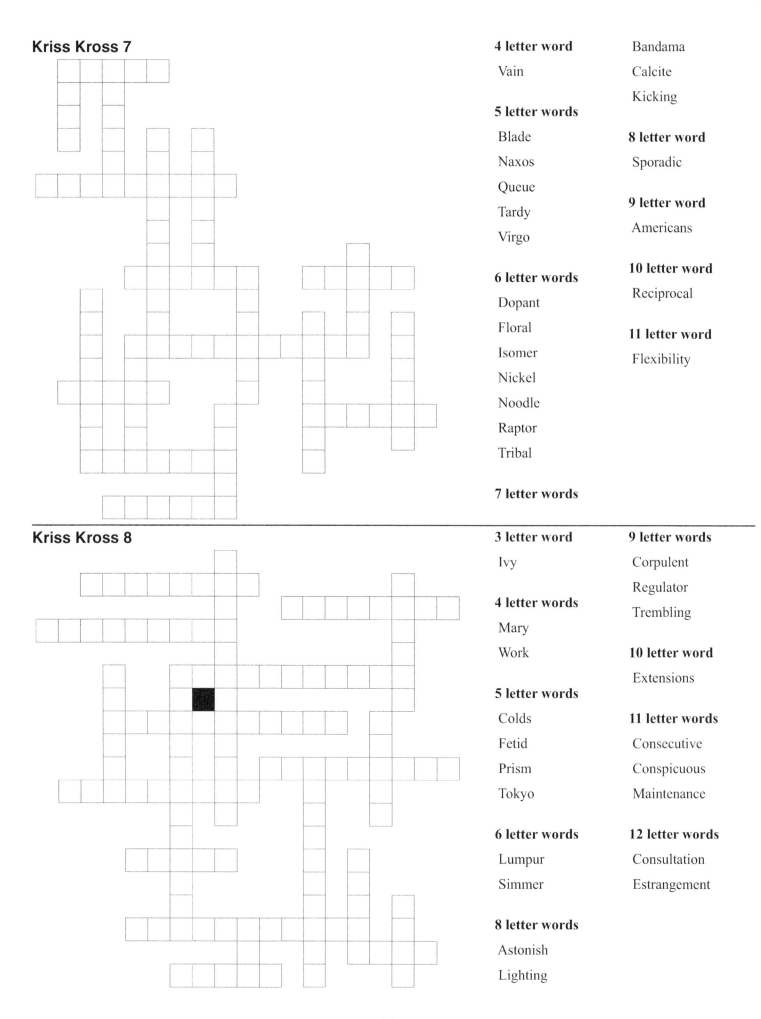

4 letter word

Vain

5 letter words

Blade

Naxos

Queue

Tardy

Virgo

6 letter words

Dopant

Floral

Isomer

Nickel

Noodle

Raptor

Tribal

7 letter words

Bandama

Calcite

Kicking

8 letter word

Sporadic

9 letter word

Americans

10 letter word

Reciprocal

11 letter word

Flexibility

Kriss Kross 8

3 letter word

Ivy

4 letter words

Mary

Work

5 letter words

Colds

Fetid

Prism

Tokyo

6 letter words

Lumpur

Simmer

8 letter words

Astonish

Lighting

9 letter words

Corpulent

Regulator

Trembling

10 letter word

Extensions

11 letter words

Consecutive

Conspicuous

Maintenance

12 letter words

Consultation

Estrangement

Kriss Kross 9

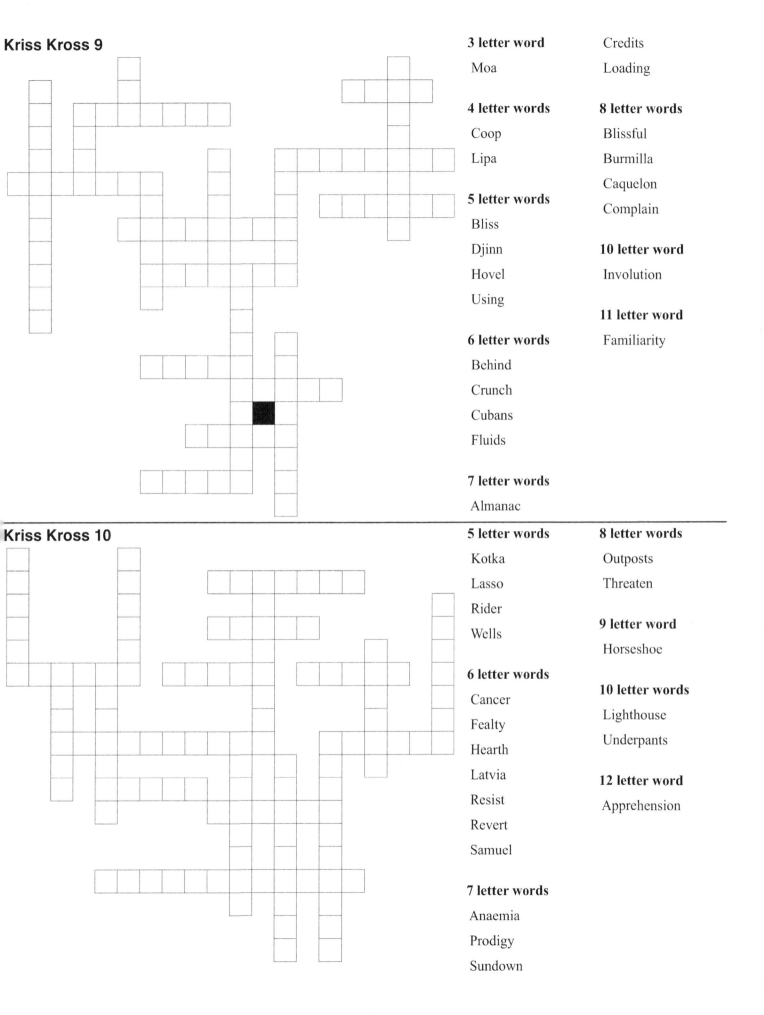

3 letter word

Moa

4 letter words

Coop

Lipa

5 letter words

Bliss

Djinn

Hovel

Using

6 letter words

Behind

Crunch

Cubans

Fluids

7 letter words

Almanac

Credits

Loading

8 letter words

Blissful

Burmilla

Caquelon

Complain

10 letter word

Involution

11 letter word

Familiarity

Kriss Kross 10

5 letter words

Kotka

Lasso

Rider

Wells

6 letter words

Cancer

Fealty

Hearth

Latvia

Resist

Revert

Samuel

7 letter words

Anaemia

Prodigy

Sundown

8 letter words

Outposts

Threaten

9 letter word

Horseshoe

10 letter words

Lighthouse

Underpants

12 letter word

Apprehension

Kriss Kross 11

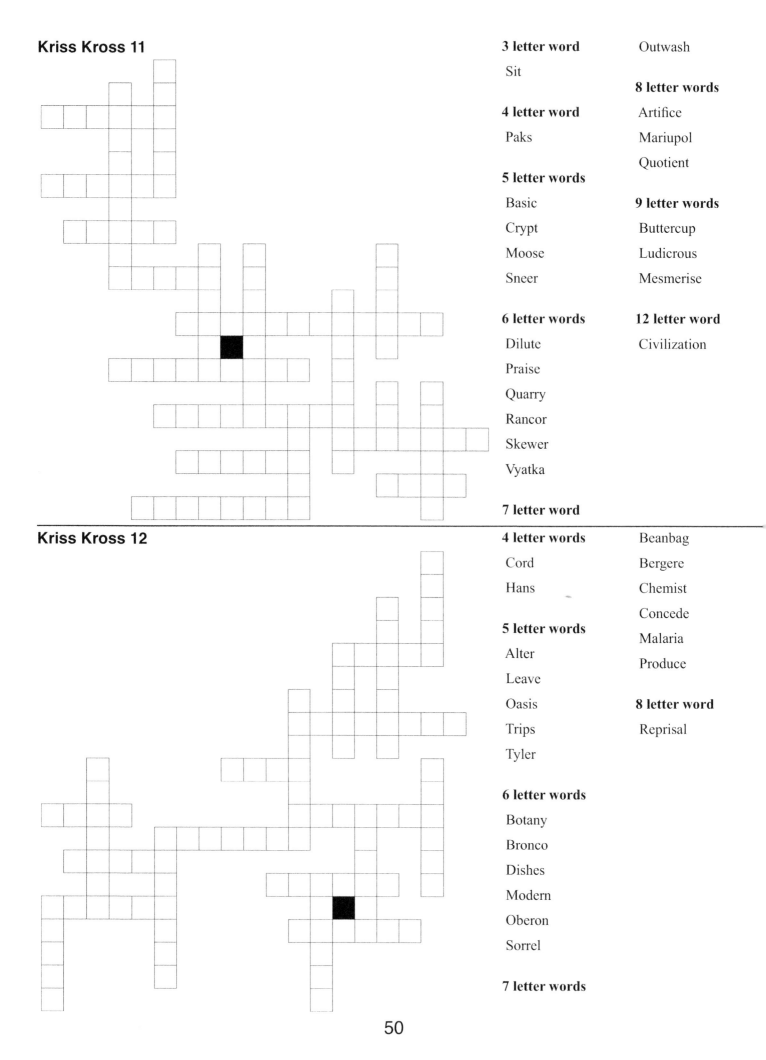

3 letter word
Sit

4 letter word
Paks

5 letter words
Basic
Crypt
Moose
Sneer

6 letter words
Dilute
Praise
Quarry
Rancor
Skewer
Vyatka

7 letter word

Outwash

8 letter words
Artifice
Mariupol
Quotient

9 letter words
Buttercup
Ludicrous
Mesmerise

12 letter word
Civilization

Kriss Kross 12

4 letter words
Cord
Hans

5 letter words
Alter
Leave
Oasis
Trips
Tyler

6 letter words
Botany
Bronco
Dishes
Modern
Oberon
Sorrel

7 letter words

Beanbag
Bergere
Chemist
Concede
Malaria
Produce

8 letter word
Reprisal

50

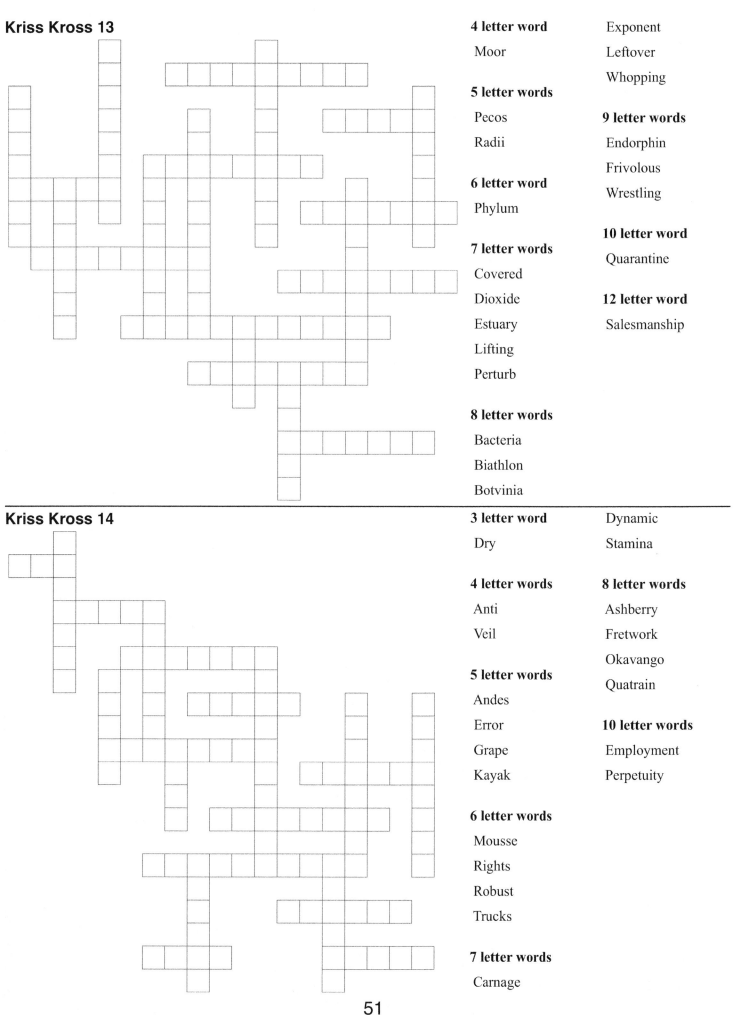

Kriss Kross 13

4 letter word
Moor

5 letter words
Pecos
Radii

6 letter word
Phylum

7 letter words
Covered
Dioxide
Estuary
Lifting
Perturb

8 letter words
Bacteria
Biathlon
Botvinia

Exponent
Leftover
Whopping

9 letter words
Endorphin
Frivolous
Wrestling

10 letter word
Quarantine

12 letter word
Salesmanship

Kriss Kross 14

3 letter word
Dry

4 letter words
Anti
Veil

5 letter words
Andes
Error
Grape
Kayak

6 letter words
Mousse
Rights
Robust
Trucks

7 letter words
Carnage

Dynamic
Stamina

8 letter words
Ashberry
Fretwork
Okavango
Quatrain

10 letter words
Employment
Perpetuity

Kriss Kross 15

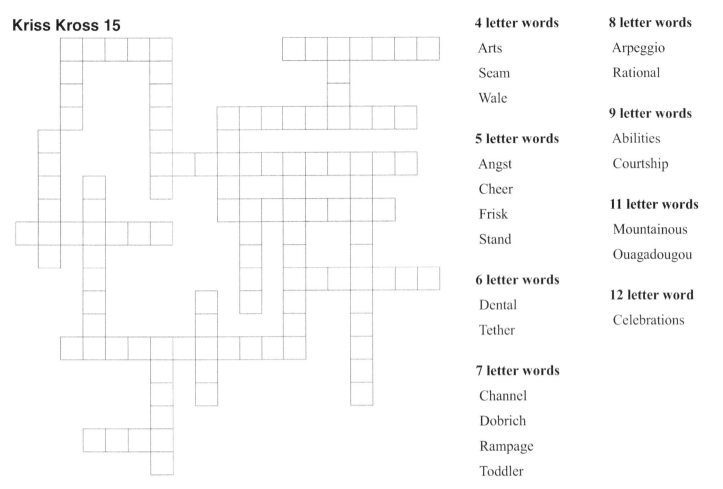

4 letter words
Arts
Seam
Wale

5 letter words
Angst
Cheer
Frisk
Stand

6 letter words
Dental
Tether

7 letter words
Channel
Dobrich
Rampage
Toddler

8 letter words
Arpeggio
Rational

9 letter words
Abilities
Courtship

11 letter words
Mountainous
Ouagadougou

12 letter word
Celebrations

Kriss Kross 16

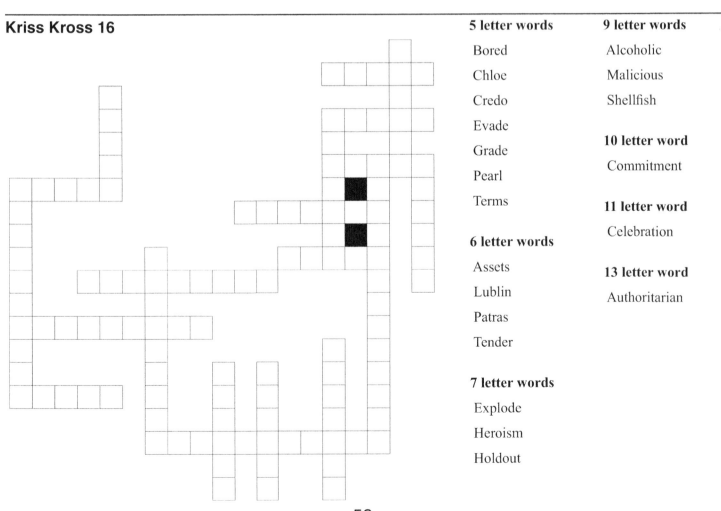

5 letter words
Bored
Chloe
Credo
Evade
Grade
Pearl
Terms

6 letter words
Assets
Lublin
Patras
Tender

7 letter words
Explode
Heroism
Holdout

9 letter words
Alcoholic
Malicious
Shellfish

10 letter word
Commitment

11 letter word
Celebration

13 letter word
Authoritarian

Kriss Kross 17

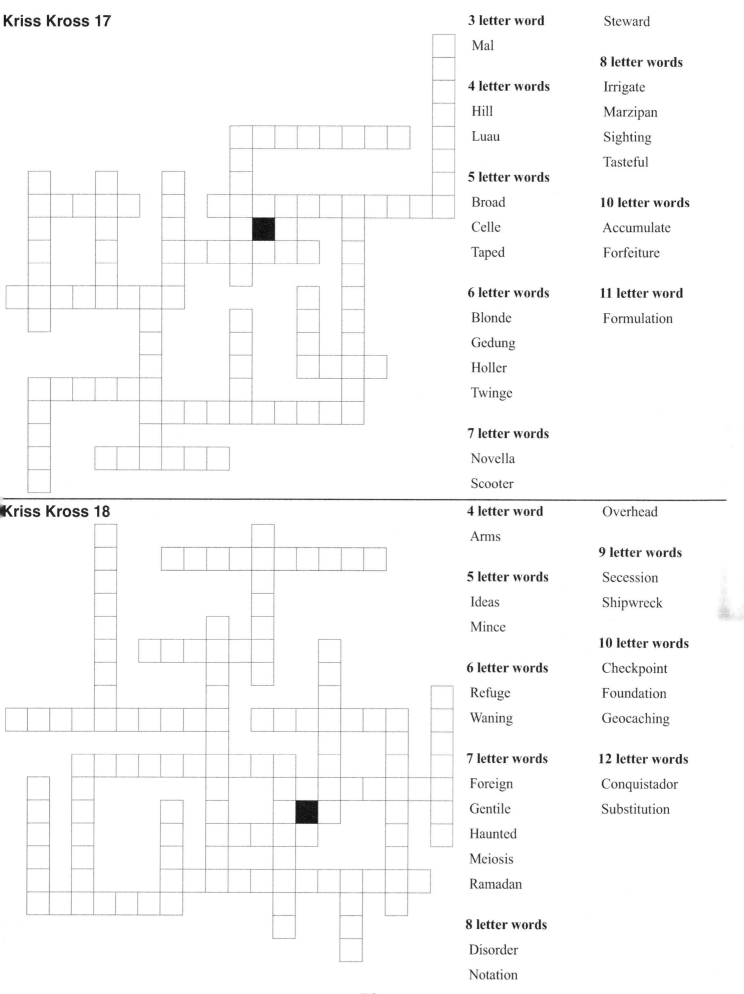

3 letter word
Mal

4 letter words
Hill
Luau

5 letter words
Broad
Celle
Taped

6 letter words
Blonde
Gedung
Holler
Twinge

7 letter words
Novella
Scooter

Steward

8 letter words
Irrigate
Marzipan
Sighting
Tasteful

10 letter words
Accumulate
Forfeiture

11 letter word
Formulation

Kriss Kross 18

4 letter word
Arms

5 letter words
Ideas
Mince

6 letter words
Refuge
Waning

7 letter words
Foreign
Gentile
Haunted
Meiosis
Ramadan

8 letter words
Disorder
Notation

Overhead

9 letter words
Secession
Shipwreck

10 letter words
Checkpoint
Foundation
Geocaching

12 letter words
Conquistador
Substitution

Codeword № 1

A puzzle grid (codeword) with numbered cells:

Row	Cells
1	7, 16, 26, 18
2	26, 2, 5, 9, 9, 1, 7, 7, 17, 26, 1, 20, 2, 22
3	1, 1, 5, 1, 20, 21, 20
4	8, 6, 1, 2, 16, 18, 1, 26, 22, 21, 13, 9, 22, 26
5	11, 19, 4, 17, 22, 11, 8
6	14, 13, 15, 26, 1, 12, 24, 20, 23, 23, 9, 22
7	3, 22, 22, 22, 18
8	4, 1, 21, 1, 2, 1, 8, 20, 24, 9, 22, 21
9	9, 26, 12, 6, 9
10	7, 1, 26, 26, 4, 6, 22, 9, 13, 22, 3, 4
11	24, 22, 13, 4, 21, 21, 13
12	10, 1, 26, 22, 6, 26, 8, 4, 12, 11, 25, 1, 9, 9
13	9, 3, 10, 5, 13, 13, 9
14	14, 22, 23, 22, 7, 22, 9, 26, 25, 4, 21, 13, 22, 6
15	26, 8, 22, 22

A B C D E F G H I J K L M N O P Q R S T U V W X Y Z

1	2	3	4	5	6	7	8	9	10	11	12	13
				Y							W	I

14	15	16	17	18	19	20	21	22	23	24	25	26

Codeword № 2

	10		10		9				1		11		4	
16	14	16	14	16	14		14	4	11	9	14	9	25	4
	11		1		4		22		14		8		9	
15	1	2	18	7	11	2	24		16	1	25	21	7	19
	7		16		21		5		6		3		19	
9	1	11	14	11	2	21	25		14	19	25	21	25	4
	19		20				10		17				5	
		19	8	13	3	14	26	14	17	2	23	25		
	12				2		16				14		5	
19	2	18	25	4	19		2	3	9	2	23	26	25	19
	21		19		9		6		4		23		10	
21	25	19	9	25	4		8	4	14	17	13	8	14	11
	23		2		2		12		21		24		3	
9	25	4	14	23	23	1	3		5	4	14	9	25	5
	5		12		11				14		3		5	

A B C D E F G H I J K L M N O P Q R S T U V W X Y Z

1	2	3	4	5	6	7	8	9	10	11	12	13
U			R	D								

14	15	16	17	18	19	20	21	22	23	24	25	26

Codeword № 3

A B C D E F G H I J K L M N O P Q R S T U V W X Y Z

1	2	3 Q	4	5	6	7	8	9	10	11 O	12	13
14	15	16	17	18	19	20	21	22	23	24 T	25	26

Codeword № 4

	2		9		23		20		12		5		3
20	17	10	7	24	15	6	15		14	5	14	16	10	23
	2		2		12		4		4		22		14
16	17	21	14	2	17		19	21	10	24	10	23	23	24
	2		1		24		7		16		23		4
16	17	23	7	22	7	14	5		14	7	24	23	10	3
			22				20		23				7
24	10	22	10	5	3	10	14	3	23	25	24	7	5	24
	2				25		11				1		
18	14	5	1	14	24		8	21	14	6	25	8	14	1
	4		17		23		9		3		23		2
16	7	12	13	26	10	10	23		10	12	7	24	10	24
	5		16		2		14		2		6		4
16	10	23	14	4	7		24	1	10	22	10	24	14	2
	3		21		14		26		11		3		5

A B C D E F G H I J K L M N O P Q R S T U V W X Y Z

1	2	3	4	5	6	7	8	9	10	11	12 G	13 W
14 A	15	16	17	18	19	20	21	22	23	24	25	26

Codeword № 5

	4	22	24	5	26	25	13	2	6	17	12	15	3	
	8		4		8	18		5		10		18		
4	4	4	8		7	4	5	5	19	23	4	13	18	21
	17		16		21		8		15		14		24	
9	18	16	8	15	26		4	15	15	26	19	18	18	7
	12				23		20		8		13		23	
21	26	9	15	18	8	8	26	8		15	15	5	8	
			2				9				16			
	4	10	4	7		23	2	4	9	21	26	10	20	26
	15		8		4		26		18				6	
9	26	1	4	8	22	22	11		19	4	8	8	26	10
	20		4		22		16		18		2		23	
7	26	9	7	10	18	17	26	24	9		4	7	26	8
	15		8		9		26		4		12		10	
	8	2	18	18	9	6	21	13	8	9	4	10	8	

A B C D E F G H I J K L M N O P Q R S T U V W X Y Z

1	2	3	4	5	6	7	8 S	9	10	11	12 K	13 G
14	15	16	17	18	19	20	21	22	23	24	25	26

Codeword № 6

17	12	24	17	4	16		1	12	22	10	12	14	5	10
	18		14		14		6		9		20		1	
13	11	24	12	17	4	20	5		12	4	13	11	6	18
	20		18		24		23		10		4		5	
		7	4	22	10	12	2	18	25	8	8	14	5	
	26		12		19		9		10			23		
15	11	17	16				3	23	12	10	1	9	5	5
	4		15		16		13		1		9		9	
23	16	5	10	16	6	5	9				4	1	1	19
	5				4		11		1		16		8	
10	12	4	24	1	18	12	1	9	4	16	15			
	16		1		11		6		23		15		5	
10	1	9	5	5	1		5	26	5	24	24	5	10	10
	11		10		14		9		9		5		21	
18	9	5	1	8	5	14	10		10	6	5	5	10	6

A B C D E F G H I J K L M N O P Q R S T U V W X Y Z

1	2	3	4	5	6	7 J	8	9	10 S	11 O	12	13
14	15	16	17	18	19	20	21	22	23	24	25	26

Codeword № 7

A B C D E F G H I J K L M N O P Q R S T U V W X Y Z

1	2	3	4	5	6	7	8	9	10	11 G	12 L	13
14	15	16	17	18 C	19	20	21	22	23	24	25	26

Codeword № 8

A B C D E F G H I J K L M N O P Q R S T U V W X Y Z

1	2	3	4	5	6	7	8	9	10	11	12	13
					A				Y	V		

14	15	16	17	18	19	20	21	22	23	24	25	26

Codeword № 9

	13		20		23		24		1		23		9	
7	26	15	9	8	9		9	11	2	12	23	9	22	22
	2		6		11		6		9		9		9	
3	11	14	24	10	18	5	19		20	14	3	3	18	15
	17		25		15		2		9		6		5	
10	4	11	1	9	8	7	16		25	2	9	6	9	16
	2						24		1		24			
5	19	1	9	18	5	12		21	9	6	16	2	25	15
			8		15		10						5	
2	8	16	9	8	5		9	16	16	2	16	25	5	12
	5		18		18		16		10		8		25	
16	20	9	15	22	5		16	5	9	4	9	6	5	6
	11		22		21		17		6		10		6	
16	9	24	5	1	5	6	5		16	14	9	6	5	12
	6		6		18		15		5		25		12	

A B C D E F G H I J K L M N O P Q R S T U V W X Y Z

1	2	3	4 F	5	6	7	8	9	10	11	12	13
14	15	16	17	18	19	20	21 V	22 Z	23	24	25	26

Codeword № 10

A B C D E F G H I J K L M N O P Q R S T U V W X Y Z

1	2	3	4	5	6	7	8	9 S	10	11	12	13
14	15	16	17	18 X	19 E	20	21	22	23	24	25	26

Codeword № 11

	21		10		19		13		17		3		13	
9	23	17	24	5	22		24	1	25	24	19	3	4	6
	12		1		2		16		9		4		10	
24	8	12	11	13	24	16	16		4	9	15	24	12	25
	26		22		12		24		4		5		24	
2	14	12	16	22	19		7	4	11	16	12	1	1	24
	12				22		22				22			
22	20	8	1	23	11	22		19	24	17	18	22	18	12
			4				9		1				25	
15	4	19	17	9	4	1	22		18	25	24	8	22	6
	9		3		26		5		24		3		2	
18	25	19	24	23	3		3	6	25	9	22	15	24	6
	9		19		6		24		12		1		15	
9	24	5	11	6	17	24	5		24	8	22	25	24	1
	25		6		22		22		5		18		6	

A B C D E F G H I J K L M N O P Q R S T U V W X Y Z

1	2	3	4	5	6	7	8 C	9	10 V	11	12	13 J
14	15	16	17	18	19	20	21	22	23	24	25	26

Codeword № 12

	22		9		19		23		20		16		10	
7	25	13	7	11	11	5	7		22	26	15	10	22	5
	13		12		22		26		5		12		11	
22	5	7	21	26	14	7	13	7	8		5	24	22	26
	7				24		12		13		16		14	
7	17	20	18	10	10		16	26	18	5	24	11	7	17
			15		22		18				16		10	
14	7	3	12	7	16	26		16	7	7	26	6	7	16
	2		14				16		10		7			
6	22	2	7	22	4	24	26		16	15	14	14	7	5
	1		4		24		22		5				16	
22	7	14	24		2	22	10	10	22	20	6	24	26	7
	14		14		7		17		2		15		6	
26	15	10	7	12	1		26	24	7	23	22	25	7	16
	10		17		25		15		16		23		14	

A B C D E F G H I J K L M N O P Q R S T U V W X Y Z

1	2	3	4	5	6	7	8	9	10	11	12	13
14	15	16	17	18	19 C	20 W	21	22	23	24	25	26 T

Codeword № 13

8	2	10	23	14	2	9	25		19	9	25	2	2	13
11		11		1		17				1		13		3
7	2	15	15	12	13	16	22		6	2	3	2	19	12
2		2		26		12				10		19		9
1	2	3	14	2	4	12	3		19	2	22	12	3	9
4		13		21		15		5		26		21		12
				19	12	25	2	26	2	20	1	2	3
25		25		1		18		21		19		20		9
26	6	3	4	2	8	6	10	11	1					
12		2		3		24		25		22		1		12
10	6	5	12	10	20		18	20	19	12	6	3	19	12
23		12		12				23		25		12		10
25	2	9	14	2	21		22	2	10	11	9	2	13	12
8		25		9				3		25		25		3
9	21	20	13	12	3		3	12	23	12	3	12	12	9

A B C D E F G H I J K L M N O P Q R S T U V W X Y Z

1	2	3	4 K	5 V	6	7	8	9	10	11	12	13 D
14	15	16	17	18	19	20	21	22	23	24	25	26

Codeword № 14

A B C D E F G H I J K L M N O P Q R S T U V W X Y Z

1	2	3	4	5	6	7	8	9	10	11	12	13
14	15	16	17 Q	18 Z	19	20 V	21	22	23	24	25	26

Codeword № 15

22	17	5	14	12	8	24	20	14	26	■	14	9	19	13
8	■	1	■	16	■	24	■	7	■	■	■	8	■	14
10	11	24	20	19	8	10	6	14	18	■	2	26	10	8
9	■	19	■	1	■	16	■	14	■	1	■	8	■	6
■	■	■	15	8	6	6	11	2	1	20	16	17	17	1
21	■	3	■	25	■	14	■	8	■	14	■	14	■	26
11	21	14	10	3	8	10	■	15	8	17	8	10	16	8
16	■	18	■	5	■	■	■	■	14	■	10	■	10
24	13	14	14	4	16	26	■	13	11	26	9	11	11	26
14	■	26	■	4	■	8	■	8	■	11	■	10	■	1
8	3	10	16	17	1	26	14	21	14	18	1	■	■	■
24	■	8	■	14	■	16	■	14	■	24	■	1	■	14
26	5	26	1	■	3	8	10	8	19	10	8	3	13	1
11	■	14	■	■	18	■	19	■	14	■	23	■	23
10	9	6	1	■	24	8	18	11	9	25	11	10	15	1

A B C D E F G H I J K L M N O P Q R S T U V W X Y Z

1	2	3	4	5	6	7	8	9	10	11	12	13
S											J	H
14	15	16	17	18	19	20	21	22	23	24	25	26

68

Codeword № 16

3	9	6	20	9	23	26	18	■	15	14	21	25	5	11
10	■	9	■	24	■	14	■	17	■	21	■	9	■	23
12	5	15	19	5	21	25	■	14	23	10	14	11	12	5
22	■	18	■	20	■	20	■	12	■	18	■	10	■	18
5	22	25	23	9	■	1	5	10	8	1	25	5	12	18
11	■	9	■	4	■	15	■	18	■	■	■	21	■	10
■	■	■	6	9	13	9	25	1	5	20	19	9	15	12
25	■	11	■	17	■	23	■	10	■	9	■	23	■	8
9	6	10	15	14	12	7	5	12	9	6	10	■	■	■
25	■	18	■	■	■	16	■	8	■	6	■	21	■	9
1	10	20	5	25	12	2	12	20	■	18	10	19	5	22
5	■	9	■	1	■	10	■	23	■	14	■	5	■	10
4	10	18	11	5	14	19	■	5	12	19	14	20	5	11
14	■	25	■	21	■	25	■	14	■	14	■	1	■	5
22	1	2	12	25	18	■	18	4	10	11	8	5	12	18

A B C D E F G H I J K L M N O P Q R S T U V W X Y Z

1	2	3	4	5	6	7	8	9	10	11	12	13
							G	O	I			

14	15	16	17	18	19	20	21	22	23	24	25	26

Codeword № 17

19	24	6	9	2	3		16	12	15	19	15	23	19	15
23		23		19			16		23		12		13
17	11	25	9	2	3		16	17	2	22	24	21	2	2
23		10		12		16		19		6		12		20
22	24	24	12		10	22	10	24	9	15	6	6	9	2
23		10		10		23		24		23		24		22
8	15	1	12	23	14	7	11	4	4	9	2			
23		2		15		12		2		23		7		12
		18	9	23	12	6	26	11	22	13	23	16	2
26		19		3		11		2		6		9		25
24	22	23	13	1	2	4	2	12	6		19	2	9	10
25		10		22		2		6		9		13		22
16	24	19	2	15	13	6	24		3	23	13	5	11	15
11		23		13		6				10		11		20
18	24	25	2	10	12	2	6		25	3	9	2	13	2

A B C D E F G H I J K L M N O P Q R S T U V W X Y Z

1 G	2	3	4	5	6	7	8	9	10	11	12	13
14	15	16	17	18	19	20 V	21	22	23	24	25	26 F

70

Codeword № 18

4	20	5	2	12	25	█	20	14	21	13	6	26	26	11
13	█	25	█	3	█	█	█	18	█	26	█	3	█	2
15	13	10	10	22	6	█	6	14	11	2	14	1	8	14
13	█	14	█	8	█	6	█	6	█	6	█	16	█	2
10	14	23	23	14	1	14	23	█	20	15	25	14	18	14
13	█	3	█	8	█	14	█	13	█	14	█	23	█	6
12	25	24	6	13	19	17	2	9	9	7	14	█	█	█
13	█	6	█	10	█	13	█	16	█	13	█	20	█	13
█	█	20	3	2	24	15	13	6	1	13	25	7	6	█
11	█	23	█	7	█	14	█	26	█	23	█	24	█	20
2	6	14	6	3	1	█	7	13	4	13	6	14	10	22
3	█	12	█	13	█	14	█	1	█	17	█	10	█	13
25	1	13	8	20	25	18	14	█	4	14	8	8	13	1
20	█	18	█	14	█	3	█	█	█	8	█	2	█	13
6	11	2	13	6	15	14	6	█	6	16	22	26	3	21

A B C D E F G H I J K L M N O P Q R S T U V W X Y Z

1 N	2	3	4	5	6	7	8	9	10	11	12	13
14	15	16	17	18	19 W	20	21	22	23	24	25 I	26

Maze № 2

Maze № 4

Maze № 6

Maze № 8

Maze № 12

Maze № 15

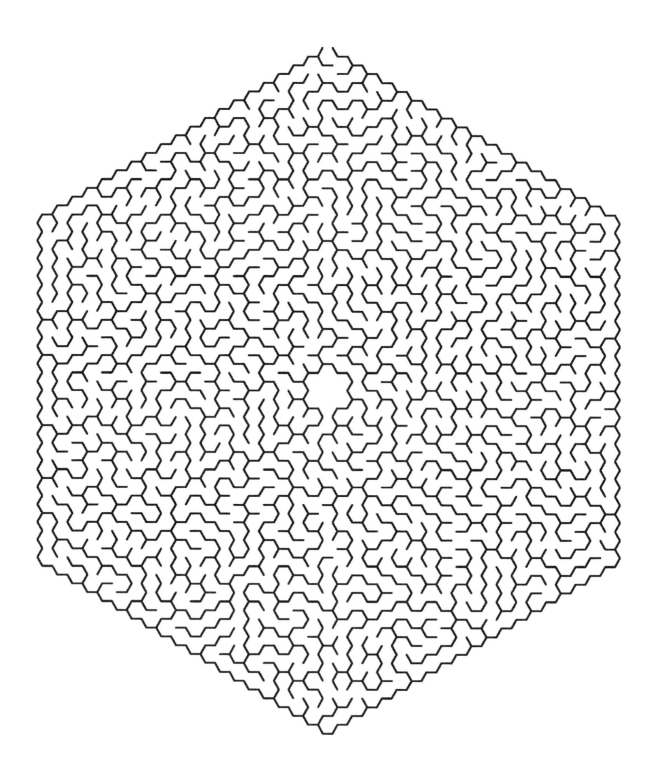

Maze № 16

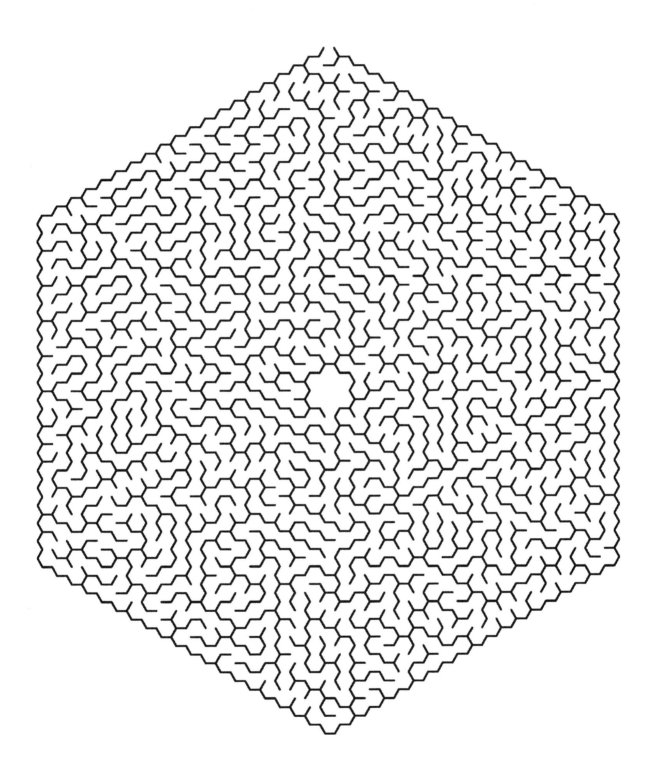

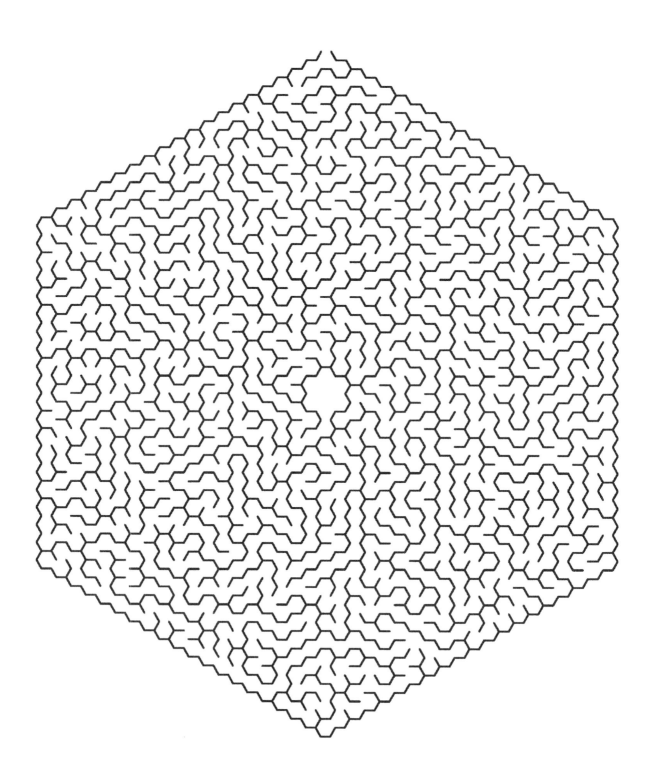

Maze № 18

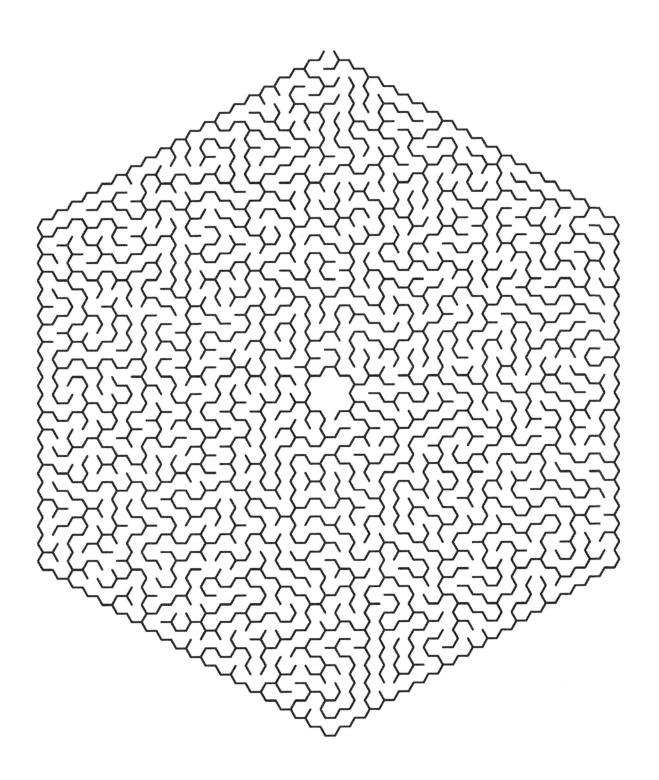

Crossword - 1

Crossword - 2

Crossword - 3

Crossword - 4

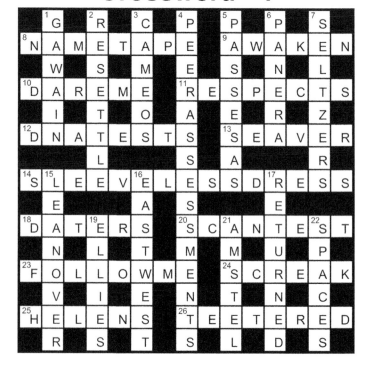

Crossword - 5

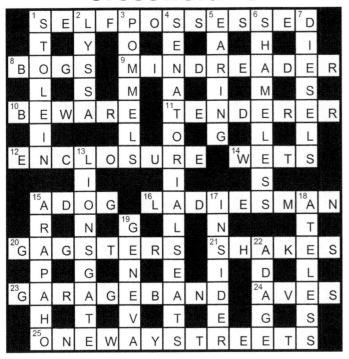

Crossword - 6

Crossword - 7

Crossword - 8

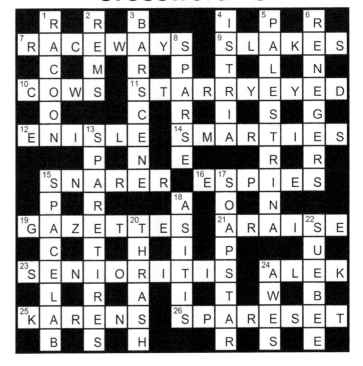

Crossword - 9

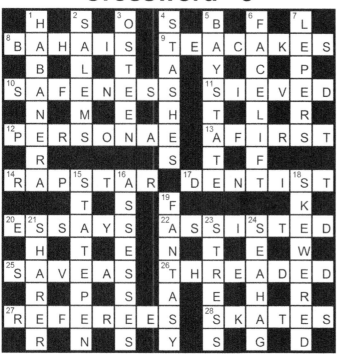

Crossword - 10

Crossword - 11

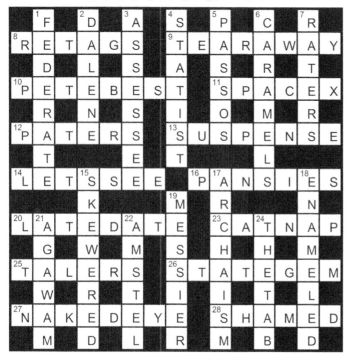

Crossword - 12

Crossword - 13

1 S	T	2 A	R	3 S	H	4 I	P	■	5 C	6 A	V	7 E	R	8 S
L	■	U	■	E	■	N	■	■	■	L	■	M	■	E
9 A	I	R	W	A	V	E	S	■	10 H	E	C	A	T	E
Y	■	O	■	C	■	L	■	■	■	H	■	N	■	S
11 E	A	R	H	O	L	E	S	■	12 S	O	N	A	T	A
D	■	A	■	W	■	G	■	13 S	■	U	■	T	■	W
■	■	■	■	■	14 M	A	D	E	A	S	C	E	N	E
15 P	■	16 B	■	17 W	■	N	■	N	■	E	■	S	■	D
18 A	D	A	G	E	N	C	I	E	S	■	■	■	■	■
S	■	K	■	R	■	E	■	G	■	19 S	■	20 S	■	21 B
22 S	I	E	G	E	L	■	23 B	A	B	A	W	A	W	A
E	■	S	■	H	■	■	■	L	■	V	■	F	■	L
24 S	L	A	K	E	S	■	25 G	E	N	E	R	A	T	E
A	■	L	■	R	■	■	■	S	■	U	■	R	■	R
26 S	P	E	W	E	R	■	27 M	E	S	S	K	I	T	S

Crossword - 14

■	1 O	2 P	E	3 R	A	4 G	L	5 A	S	6 S	E	7 S	■	■
8 U	■	L	■	E	■	R	■	S	■	L	■	I	■	9 B
10 S	H	A	K	I	R	A	■	11 S	E	A	H	A	R	E
U	■	Y	■	S	■	S	■	E	■	W	■	M	■	L
12 A	L	E	C	S	■	■	13 N	E	W	S	R	E	E	L
L	■	R	■	U	■	14 C	■	N	■	■	■	S	■	E
15 S	I	S	T	E	R	H	O	O	D	■	16 O	E	D	S
U	■	■	■	S	■	R	■	N	■	17 K	■	■	■	L
18 S	E	19 A	S	■	20 T	O	E	T	H	E	L	21 I	N	E
P	■	D	■	■	■	M	■	V	■	N	■	M	■	T
22 E	M	A	N	23 A	T	E	D	■	■	24 S	L	A	N	T
C	■	G	■	B	■	D	■	25 W	■	T	■	G	■	R
26 T	R	I	B	O	R	O	■	27 A	P	A	T	I	T	E
S	■	O	■	I	■	M	■	Y	■	R	■	N	■	S
■	■	28 S	I	L	V	E	R	S	C	R	E	E	N	■

Crossword - 15

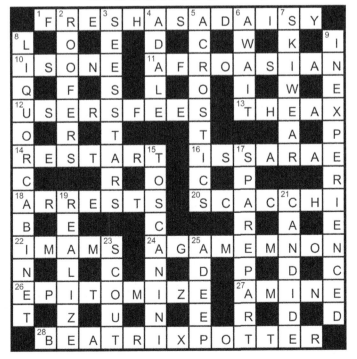

■	1 F	2 R	E	3 S	H	4 A	S	5 A	D	6 A	I	7 S	Y	■
8 L	■	O	■	E	■	D	■	C	■	W	■	K	■	9 I
10 I	S	O	N	E	■	11 A	F	R	O	A	S	I	A	N
Q	■	F	■	S	■	L	■	O	■	I	■	W	■	E
12 U	S	E	R	S	F	E	E	S	■	13 T	H	E	A	X
O	■	R	■	T	■	■	■	T	■	■	■	A	■	P
14 R	E	S	T	A	R	15 T	■	16 I	S	17 S	A	R	A	E
C	■	■	■	R	■	O	■	C	■	P	■	■	■	R
18 A	R	19 R	E	S	T	S	■	20 S	C	A	C	21 C	H	I
B	■	E	■	■	■	C	■	■	■	R	■	A	■	E
22 I	M	A	M	23 S	■	24 A	G	25 A	M	E	M	N	O	N
N	■	L	■	C	■	N	■	D	■	P	■	D	■	C
26 E	P	I	T	O	M	I	Z	E	■	27 A	M	I	N	E
T	■	Z	■	U	■	N	■	E	■	R	■	D	■	D
■	28 B	E	A	T	R	I	X	P	O	T	T	E	R	■

Crossword - 16

1 S	E	2 A	S	3 O	N	4 P	A	5 S	S	■	6 E	7 S	C	8 E
R	■	S	■	C	■	R	■	I	■	■	■	N	■	A
9 A	B	O	V	E	W	A	T	E	R	■	10 C	A	V	S
S	■	R	■	A	■	Y	■	R	■	11 E	■	K	■	Y
■	■	■	12 I	N	R	E	T	R	O	S	P	E	C	T
13 S	■	14 P	■	S	■	R	■	A	■	C	■	R	■	A
15 A	B	A	S	E	R	S	■	16 S	T	A	G	I	E	R
N	■	P	■	L	■	■	■	■	■	P	■	V	■	G
17 T	H	E	R	E	S	18 A	■	19 T	H	E	R	E	S	E
A	■	R	■	V	■	D	■	V	■	C	■	R	■	T
20 M	I	C	H	E	L	A	N	G	E	L	O	■	■	■
A	■	H	■	N	■	Y	■	U	■	A	■	21 H	■	22 A
23 R	I	A	A	■	24 C	A	P	I	T	U	L	A	T	E
I	■	S	■	■	■	G	■	D	■	S	■	V	■	R
25 A	P	E	D	■	26 R	O	S	E	P	E	T	A	L	S

Crossword - 17

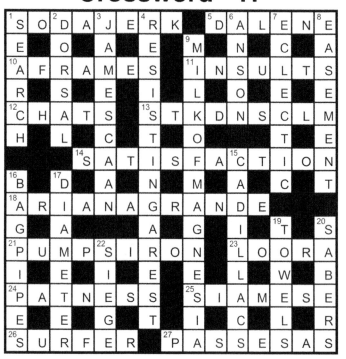

Crossword - 18

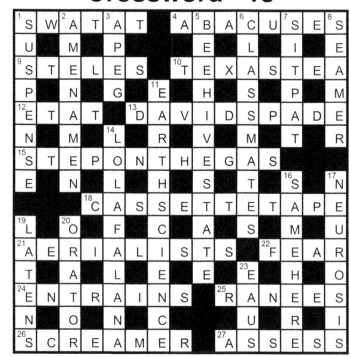

Sudoku - 1

6	2	8	1	9	3	7	5	4
9	5	3	2	7	4	8	6	1
1	4	7	8	5	6	9	2	3
3	9	1	6	4	7	2	8	5
2	7	6	3	8	5	1	4	9
4	8	5	9	2	1	3	7	6
5	1	4	7	3	8	6	9	2
7	3	9	4	6	2	5	1	8
8	6	2	5	1	9	4	3	7

Sudoku - 2

2	4	8	9	5	7	1	6	3
7	3	9	2	1	6	8	5	4
5	1	6	4	3	8	2	9	7
9	7	3	1	6	4	5	8	2
6	5	4	8	9	2	3	7	1
1	8	2	3	7	5	9	4	6
3	6	7	5	2	9	4	1	8
8	9	1	7	4	3	6	2	5
4	2	5	6	8	1	7	3	9

Sudoku - 3

4	5	9	8	7	2	1	3	6
2	8	1	9	6	3	4	5	7
3	7	6	5	1	4	8	2	9
7	1	4	6	3	9	5	8	2
5	2	8	7	4	1	6	9	3
6	9	3	2	5	8	7	1	4
8	3	7	1	2	6	9	4	5
9	4	5	3	8	7	2	6	1
1	6	2	4	9	5	3	7	8

Sudoku - 4

2	6	1	7	3	8	9	4	5
8	4	5	2	6	9	3	1	7
3	9	7	4	1	5	8	2	6
4	7	2	3	5	1	6	9	8
9	1	8	6	7	2	5	3	4
6	5	3	9	8	4	1	7	2
1	2	4	5	9	6	7	8	3
5	3	9	8	2	7	4	6	1
7	8	6	1	4	3	2	5	9

Sudoku - 5

3	4	6	9	8	1	5	7	2
9	1	5	2	6	7	3	4	8
2	8	7	5	4	3	9	1	6
1	9	4	3	2	8	6	5	7
6	7	8	1	5	9	2	3	4
5	2	3	6	7	4	8	9	1
7	3	9	8	1	2	4	6	5
8	6	1	4	9	5	7	2	3
4	5	2	7	3	6	1	8	9

Sudoku - 6

8	5	2	3	7	9	1	6	4
3	6	1	5	8	4	2	7	9
9	7	4	2	1	6	3	5	8
6	3	5	1	4	7	8	9	2
2	8	9	6	5	3	7	4	1
1	4	7	8	9	2	6	3	5
7	1	8	4	3	5	9	2	6
4	2	3	9	6	8	5	1	7
5	9	6	7	2	1	4	8	3

Sudoku - 7

6	4	5	1	3	8	9	7	2
8	1	7	5	9	2	4	3	6
2	3	9	4	6	7	8	5	1
4	2	8	6	7	1	3	9	5
5	6	3	9	8	4	2	1	7
9	7	1	2	5	3	6	8	4
7	5	6	8	4	9	1	2	3
3	9	2	7	1	6	5	4	8
1	8	4	3	2	5	7	6	9

Sudoku - 8

5	8	7	4	2	3	1	6	9
1	9	2	5	6	7	4	8	3
4	3	6	8	9	1	2	5	7
9	6	1	7	8	5	3	4	2
7	5	4	2	3	9	6	1	8
3	2	8	1	4	6	9	7	5
2	4	3	6	5	8	7	9	1
6	1	5	9	7	2	8	3	4
8	7	9	3	1	4	5	2	6

Sudoku - 9

9	4	5	1	8	7	6	2	3
1	2	3	6	5	9	4	7	8
7	6	8	4	2	3	9	1	5
5	1	6	7	4	2	8	3	9
3	7	2	8	9	5	1	4	6
8	9	4	3	1	6	2	5	7
6	8	1	5	3	4	7	9	2
4	5	9	2	7	8	3	6	1
2	3	7	9	6	1	5	8	4

Sudoku - 10

3	2	9	5	1	4	7	6	8
6	4	5	2	8	7	1	3	9
7	1	8	9	3	6	5	2	4
4	7	6	3	2	1	8	9	5
1	5	2	6	9	8	4	7	3
9	8	3	7	4	5	6	1	2
2	6	7	4	5	9	3	8	1
5	9	1	8	6	3	2	4	7
8	3	4	1	7	2	9	5	6

Sudoku - 11

7	3	4	8	9	6	2	1	5
8	5	2	1	3	7	6	9	4
9	6	1	5	4	2	7	3	8
5	9	3	6	2	4	1	8	7
1	2	6	7	5	8	9	4	3
4	7	8	9	1	3	5	2	6
2	8	9	3	6	5	4	7	1
3	1	5	4	7	9	8	6	2
6	4	7	2	8	1	3	5	9

Sudoku - 12

3	8	1	4	6	9	5	7	2
7	4	6	2	1	5	9	8	3
2	9	5	3	8	7	1	6	4
8	6	9	5	7	2	3	4	1
5	2	4	1	3	6	8	9	7
1	7	3	8	9	4	6	2	5
6	1	2	7	5	8	4	3	9
4	3	8	9	2	1	7	5	6
9	5	7	6	4	3	2	1	8

Sudoku - 13

4	9	8	7	6	1	5	3	2
3	6	5	4	2	9	8	7	1
7	1	2	5	3	8	9	4	6
5	4	6	1	8	7	2	9	3
8	2	9	3	4	5	1	6	7
1	7	3	6	9	2	4	8	5
6	8	1	2	7	4	3	5	9
2	3	4	9	5	6	7	1	8
9	5	7	8	1	3	6	2	4

Sudoku - 14

4	5	9	3	1	7	6	2	8
2	3	6	8	5	9	4	7	1
8	1	7	4	2	6	9	3	5
3	7	4	5	6	2	8	1	9
1	2	5	9	7	8	3	6	4
9	6	8	1	3	4	7	5	2
5	4	2	6	9	3	1	8	7
6	9	1	7	8	5	2	4	3
7	8	3	2	4	1	5	9	6

Sudoku - 15

6	1	8	3	5	7	9	2	4
5	7	4	2	9	8	3	1	6
3	9	2	1	4	6	7	8	5
9	6	1	7	8	4	5	3	2
4	5	3	6	1	2	8	9	7
2	8	7	9	3	5	6	4	1
7	4	5	8	2	9	1	6	3
8	3	6	4	7	1	2	5	9
1	2	9	5	6	3	4	7	8

Sudoku - 16

7	9	5	3	8	1	2	4	6
6	1	8	2	7	4	3	9	5
4	2	3	9	6	5	8	1	7
8	7	2	1	4	6	9	5	3
5	4	6	8	9	3	7	2	1
1	3	9	5	2	7	4	6	8
2	6	4	7	5	8	1	3	9
3	5	7	4	1	9	6	8	2
9	8	1	6	3	2	5	7	4

Sudoku - 17

7	5	6	2	8	1	9	4	3
4	3	9	6	5	7	2	1	8
8	2	1	4	9	3	7	5	6
5	6	4	1	2	9	8	3	7
2	7	3	5	4	8	1	6	9
9	1	8	3	7	6	5	2	4
3	4	7	9	1	5	6	8	2
1	8	2	7	6	4	3	9	5
6	9	5	8	3	2	4	7	1

Sudoku - 18

4	3	9	5	7	8	1	6	2
8	1	5	4	6	2	3	9	7
7	2	6	3	1	9	8	4	5
5	9	2	6	8	1	7	3	4
3	6	8	7	2	4	9	5	1
1	4	7	9	3	5	6	2	8
2	5	3	8	9	7	4	1	6
6	7	1	2	4	3	5	8	9
9	8	4	1	5	6	2	7	3

Word Search - 1

Word Search - 2

Word Search - 3

Word Search - 4

Word Search - 5

```
S G E O R G E T T E P F A S Q
H U B M M A G A Z I N E S N G
E R Z U U H P S D O O C T N J
N H V N W C U F K Z I M I K S
Z O R D B K U U I R P G Y M L
H L J J R C S N T S G R E O C
E L H A O P H C H O C L O M G
N Y B M T C E I L A B A D A H
G W R E H L L B C O P J L R E
L O S N E K E W R K I P Q S I
O O O A R P H P Y D C L Y U R
E D E X S A S Y S I R A I P E
S T R A N S M I S S I O N I S
S P H O T O G R A P H S W A S
I N H I B I T O R U D D R L G
```

Word Search - 6

```
H Y P O T H E S I S J G M J G
W E S C O F U V U B N G P B P
F L T O B E K V E I N S D P H
W T R N T W N N K I M C F M Y
A L E T C O I O T M A D Y L S
T I P R Q H R H A O X F D D I
T C I I S T C D H R I T E E C
E E D B S A R G G L L Q M P I
N N A U Y S H O V E L S C R A
T S T A O K A P I A F U E N
I I I I N I K O L A E V B S Q
O N O O P T I C I A N E S S H
N G N N R E F E R R A L S I J
A S H L O R G A N I Z E X O B
D I L E T T A N T E B R Y N X
```

Word Search - 7

```
Q C D D C T W H I T N E Y D V
U A E I X R M Z H C V O V I U
A T B A V E B O Y I K P O C R
D A A L N L A E T F H T Q T U
R F U O K A G E L U S C S A I
I A C G M X R I I F R X A T N
L L H U I C X N U J A J M E O
A Q E E C A K S U R S D K N
T U R S L H E V O N N T T B C
E E Y K C E W E F T L E E C H
R X Y A N M S A R A G R A R A
A U H P C I U S E E J M Y Q L
L C P A R S I M O N I O U S A
P E A C E E E G A N A C H E N
B E S P R I T V B P R J U G T
```

Word Search - 8

```
D U P R Y P S D J C I M J U V
M I T T E N S S T A R A E N Z
S N V J X I A U S E L N M L W
G I T O D F O S W O F D R E V
O N R N H Y A O N B S M I A X
H N O G A K L A E I I S P S E
V I U L L F R D O U B T S H X
I N G E N G A G I T A T I O N
G G H U E D P Y I N P I B T J
O S S R P R O C E D U R E S M
R H I S T O R I C A L M G Q S
P A C I F I S T K F A Q C F L
X O E U R A S I A S S U I R E
X N Y K Q H C Q G D M D O V E
P F A D P M Y U O E R J G N P
```

Word Search - 9

```
F N O N A L C O H O L I C K Q
O A D E C O M P O S E D K N S
L N I N E F F E C T U A L L Y
K N O O F G G R E E N L A N D
L U C A N I A E V S P Q N O G
O L O M U R S I I N N O G N E
R M D Z V E A T I Z I R I K T
E E Z Y R W I R B T E R N H T
N N A O M R T Z A D E N K R Y
S T F J T S C T N E I R O N S
A B U N A N N U N B Q Q Z X B
I F A G D E M I T A S S E Y U
Z K Z C M Z G S D V M I A D R
M I G A O N H M E M B E R S G
M N L F E P V P I R A T E T F
```

Word Search - 10

```
P R O V I D E R B A N E P V B
C R E F L I D K C S O D R T U
O A P P G S J A P N T L E N L
N S I Y R T N C C N C D C A L
M T T E A R P U L P I T A P E
K O O H A U M W T L P U R P T
A U M L J S A N A Q S H I R P
R N E O S T E V C L P T O A R
L D L N V R N J S U K J U I O
U X A O E I B R R I M E S S F
K E D F P R E S I D U E R E F
J M F U R F W U T Z H A A S M
R I T P E K I P U W W I P Z A
D Y L Y T B F H A G A P Z X B
M V V I Q T E L L E R Z P I V
```

Word Search - 11

```
S F O R T U I T O U S Y K T X
H D U C K L I N G L H E N T L
O R O O M M A T E P G E P A F
R I M K O W J J A D D J T M W
T F I T K T I R I N C I T K D
C B L O Q Q G R U B G Y J F T
U C I P H O T M E I V S Z V D
T O T M I R G V D S O M U S G
S N A B A I P F S T A F F T S
A J N P S J K M D Z U E W A W
T U T U Q V D C E V F Y F I E
C R E A T I O N N T R E U N E
Y E J D O M I N I C A D V E K
A S P I C E X V M W Y J X D O
E C O M P A T I B I L I T Y A
```

Word Search - 12

```
C O N T R O V E R S Y P L A U
V N W E P S U B S I D Y L N M
I B E W G B G R E A T E R T G
G O K S K O P E L O S L M E E
N R V A T Z D E R Y A M W E T
E D D I H E G P H T I D M A H
T E R K L E A C N T D I A S A
E N S T L K R E I O Y O Y N N
O O W G I S W S D L O L T E
O O O W G I S W S D L O L T O
M C E I T J T P D Y I M Y O E
B R L N U A K C D Q C O R R U
U O O V Z M C O H L R L B M A
Q C O R R E C T I O N A B S O
G R A V E Y A R D K G E F T R
```

102

Word Search - 13

Word Search - 14

Word Search - 15

Word Search - 16

Word Search - 17

```
T W R E G I S T R A T I O N X
H V D O M I N A T E E E O Y V
D I E S T A N D O U T I T F O
S B T R F B N A T I O N S U L
Y B D O B Y H H I U B C S K E
B R E A K A W A Y M N W Z A R
T Y X P H R L T M O M E N T F
S M I R A G E L C Z V N S Z B
O L G K C K C S Y P O L L O I
Z R E M E M B E R I N G C X R
O H O R R I F I C F P Y T V D
P N E U M O C O N I O S I S Q
O B D S E E D L I N G S N G F
L E A F H O P P E R S I I T H
S A L V A T O R E P K Z C L E
```

Word Search - 18

```
D E L I C A T E S S E N G P J
P E P P E R S D C Y F O R T Y
C M S S X S A Y O K F X D T D
L Z B V Y R I W T C N H V A S
A J E P T O S U I O M U Q P W
N H D N P A O J L U A G U S K
D R R D R B M Q L N C P G C T
E X O U E S E M I T P Z A A G
S O O Y S U T R O E A Z L R M
T F M E E R R A N R N Q H V T
I K B U N D Y B C F T C S E B
N W W L T S V B Z E H Z T S O
E C R Y S T A L S I E C A E V
M A P H R A O E D T R I B H U
Y M F X E R Q U E E N S S P O
```

Kriss Kross - 1

Kriss Kross - 2

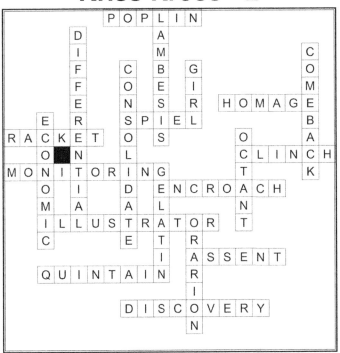

Kriss Kross - 3

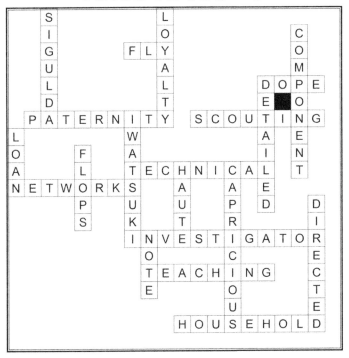

Kriss Kross - 4

Kriss Kross - 5

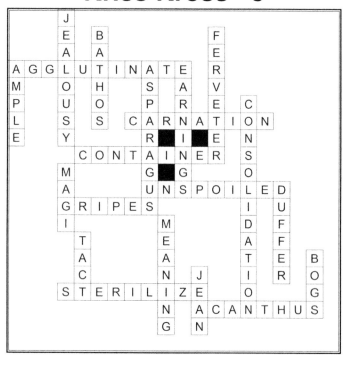

Kriss Kross - 6

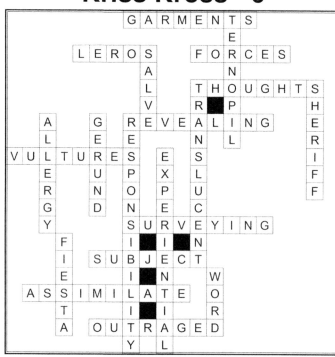

Kriss Kross - 7

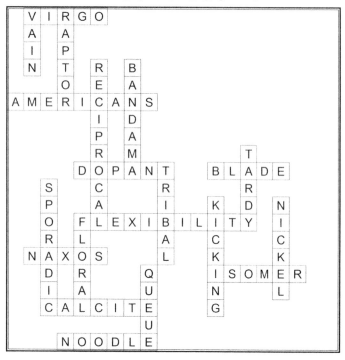

Kriss Kross - 8

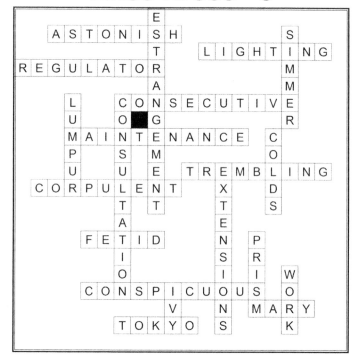

Kriss Kross - 9

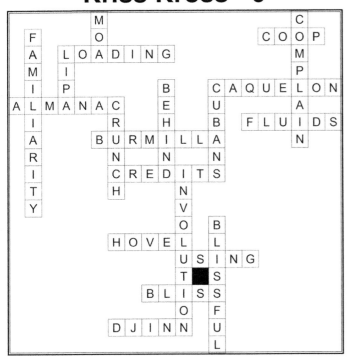

Kriss Kross - 10

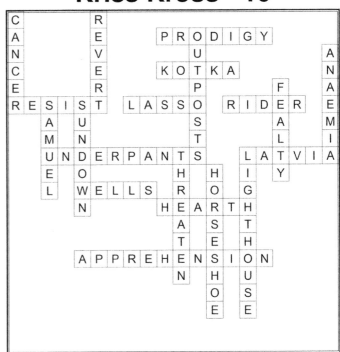

Kriss Kross - 11

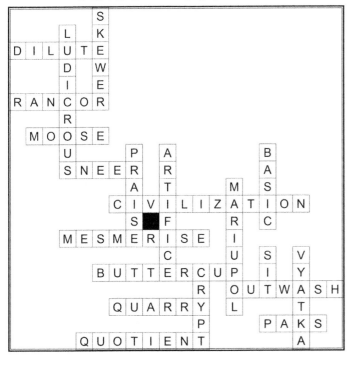

Kriss Kross - 12

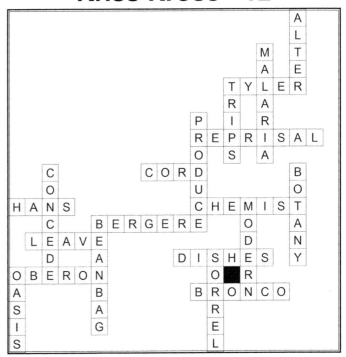

Kriss Kross - 13

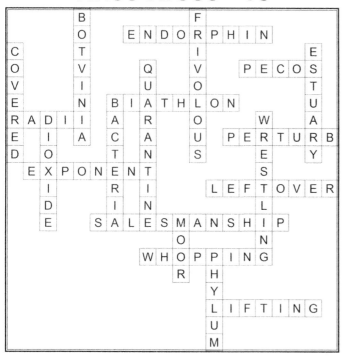

Kriss Kross - 14

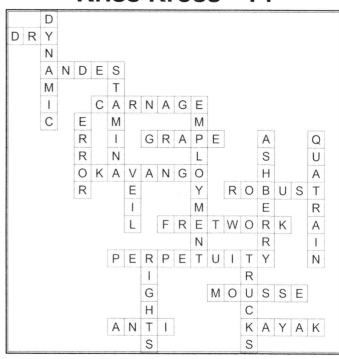

Kriss Kross - 15

Kriss Kross - 16

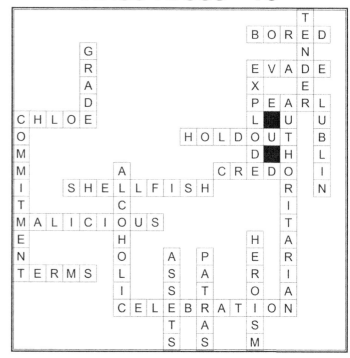

Kriss Kross - 17

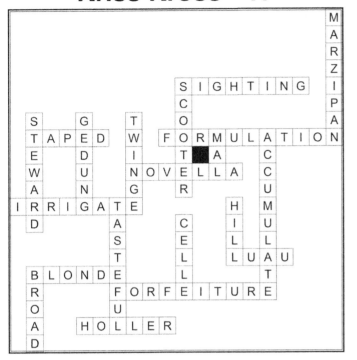

Kriss Kross - 18

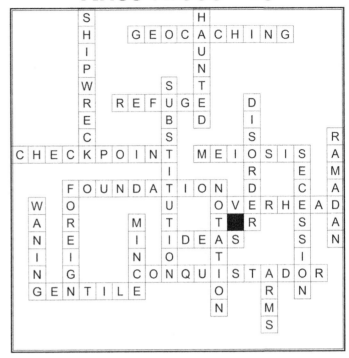

Codeword - 1

Codeword - 2

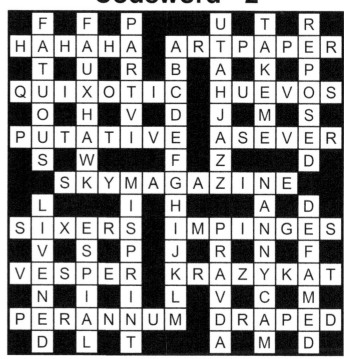

Codeword - 3

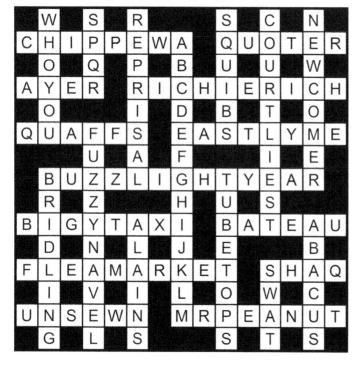

Codeword - 4

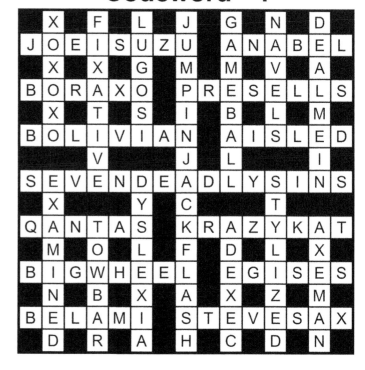

Codeword - 5

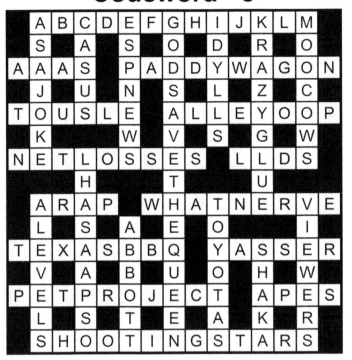

Codeword - 6

Codeword - 7

Codeword - 8

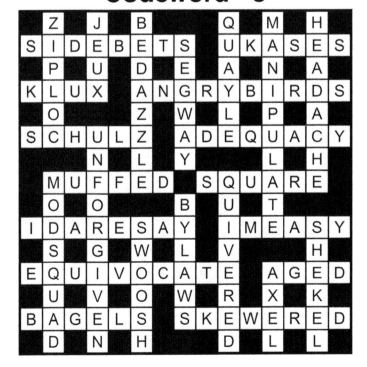

Codeword - 9

Codeword - 10

Codeword - 11

Codeword - 12

Codeword - 13

Codeword - 14

Codeword - 15

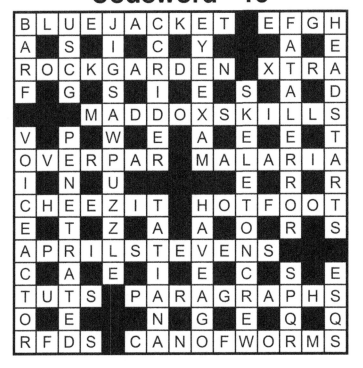

Codeword - 16

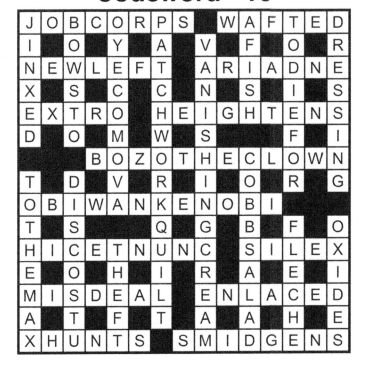

Codeword - 17

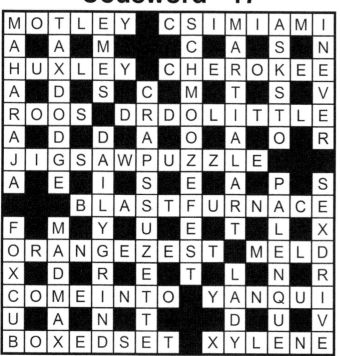

Codeword - 18

Maze - 1

Maze - 2

Maze - 3

Maze - 4

Maze - 5

Maze - 6

Maze - 7

Maze - 8

Maze - 9

Maze - 10

Maze - 11

Maze - 12

Maze - 13

Maze - 14

Maze - 15

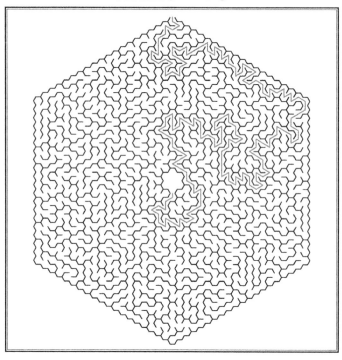

Maze - 16

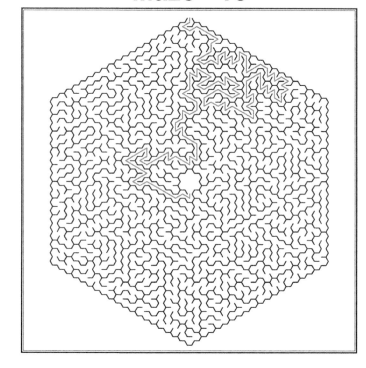

Maze - 17

Maze - 18

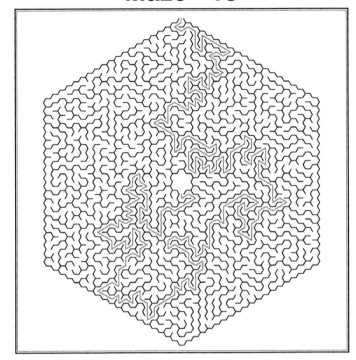

BONUS!

1

		9	7					
5	3		2					
		8	5			3		
7								9
8	5		9			1		
					1			4
		3				5		8
1	7					4		
			4	2			6	

2

	9							
	7					3		
		2	5	4				
		1			5		6	4
							5	
	8				1			3
		9			6		4	
		6	9					1
		4		8				7

3

				9				
3				5		1	7	
4		1	6			2		
7				4		9	6	
5		6						8
	2					4		
	5				3		2	
1		8		5				
			7		3			

4

						6		2
		4				8		
5						4		
				6				3
	4		2	1	3		6	9
	5							
6		3		9	7			
	7				4			
				3	1			7

5

5								2
1	7			9				
			6		2			
	9	5						4
			8	1		3		
		6						
6					8	1		
			5			8	4	
					7			3

6

	2			6				
			7			6		
	8	6	4	1			2	
		5				8		
			8	3		4		
						2		5
	4	9				1		
7			9					6
		1			4			7

120

7

	7	8	6				5	
			2					3
6					8			4
5			9	2			6	
		3	5		4			
				6				
8								7
		6				9	4	
1		9	4					

8

7	6			1				
		5				6		1
		3			9		2	
9			1	8	3			5
						9	4	
	1		4					
8	7				5			3
5				7				

9

		9						
				8	7			6
3	7			5				
9	8	4						
			8					
				4		2		1
5	9				6	2		
1		6	9					5
2								7

10

		3	2					
							7	
	5				8			
		4				6		
4			5	9	7			
1	3		7			2		
7		8		4				
	9	5			8	1		
	2			3				

11

		5		4				
2					1			
	4	7		1				2
7				8	4	6		
8			7					
		1						3
4		3				8		
		9	2				3	
		8			5		2	

12

						6		
9		4				5		7
	5	2			1	8		
3								
			6			1		4
			1		7			
5	1			3		2	9	
								5
6		8		2				

BONUS!

13

	8			7			6	
5						1	4	
			2					9
		9				6		4
3							7	
			2	6			8	1
		8	4		6			
2								
	7	4	8				1	

14

							3	
			4			5		6
1	3		6			7		8
		6						
			5	2	8			
2	9				4			
5	6							7
	2	3						9
			1		7		2	

15

			9					
	6		4					
			6	8	9			
	4					7		8
5				1				
		9		5		3	4	
2					1			5
1					7	8		6
	5							7

16

					7	9		
8	3						1	
			9			2	6	
6			9					
1	2		3					
3				6			5	
			4			5		
7	8					9	6	
				7	8	4		

17

9								
	2	7					4	
4			3			6	7	
	8	5		6	7	2	1	
		2						4
			5	2		7		
			1	4		5		
			9	5				
	4							

18

4	6					3	5	
			8	1				
2								
			2					
1	8				5	6		
	5					8		
	9		4					3
8				3	1	6	7	
				1	4			

BONUS!

19

			8				7	2
	6		1					
		3	2			4		
		6			3			
				1		9		
8			7		6			
		8				5	1	
	2		3				7	
7	3	5						

20

3			9					
6		1						
	2				7			4
		4		2	3			
						5		1
				4	5			3
	8	9	3					5
		2	6	9			1	
						9		

21

	8			6				
7						1		
				4				5
2	5	3		9				
		8	6		3		4	
			7					
3				2			8	
	4					6		3
					8	7		

22

7								4
8						1		7
			5	4		2		
			4	3	7			
	9						4	3
	6	9			8			
				9				
	3			2				
					8	9		2

23

		7				8	2	
5	3					7		
	4							
		9	2		1	5		
3					6			
6			8				1	
	8				4	7		
		3	9	5				
			8					

24

1	9						7	
			1	2				4
3	2			9		4		6
		6			3	7		
8			6					3
5						9	8	
2		4					3	
				5	8	6		

BONUS!

25

	2	5						
				7		6		
			5	8				9
5								
	3			6			8	
6	8			3	9			
		9						
			1		2	3		
			6	4		1		8

26

					8			1
6	7				4			5
	3		9					
						6	1	
				5			3	
		8	2					9
	6			8			2	4
			7	2	1			
9						5		

27

			8		3		9	
								6
3			4			2		
	2				6			
	7			4		3	2	
	8		5			4		
8			1		9			
6	1			2				9
					7			

28

		1	4		3			
			8				6	
7		3		9			8	
				4	1			
		2				1		
	5	7					2	
	2					6		
						3		
6				3	5	9		

29

		1		9			2	
8								
	7			2	5			3
2				6	1	9		5
					6			7
	8							
	9	8	4			2		
	5	4			3			
			5			3		

30

						3		
				1		8	6	2
2		3		4				
				6				
	8			3	5		2	
3							9	
		7			2			1
	1		3	8		9		
9				7			5	

BONUS!

31

7	8	2		4				1
6		9			7			
				3				
3								
	1	4	5		7			2
		6			9			
			6	1			8	3
			3		6			
				9	2			

32

		6	4			1		
				8	9			3
								6
				7	8	2		
7	1					6		
		9			6			
8				2			1	5
					4	9		
	2				7			

33

2		6		3		8		
			8		4			
		4		7			5	
			7					
					6		8	2
6	1	3	2					
	5		1	2				
			4			2		
1								7

34

		5	3		6			
	7			4				
4			9			8		
				7	3		9	
					2		1	
6	1							
2		7				3		9
		9		6		2		
								8

35

6			3			7		
		9		4	1			
								8
1		4		3	2		5	6
		3						
			8			1		
	6				5			
					2			
2	9		1		6			5

36

3				5			4	
		2			8			
5	9		6	2		1		
		7		4				
		8		3		6		
						7	4	
							8	2
7		5	1					9

BONUS!

37

8	7			1				9
9			4					
	5							
	6							
7	2						4	
		5		8		2	7	
		6	3					
				5	2		1	
							8	6

38

						8		
	7		9			5	4	2
		8	3			9	7	
2							6	
	6			4				
	8	4			9			3
7	2	3			1			
	9		8		7		5	

39

			2		3		4	6
				5				
5	4		7					2
8					6			4
	3	4	8					
9		6				2	7	
		9					3	
					9			
			5	2	7			

40

	1							
	2	3		4				5
5				6			2	
	6		9					
8			1		3		9	4
	3			7		1		
	9					2		6
1		8						
							7	3

41

6			9				8	4
	2			1	3			
9		1	6			7		
			5		6		7	
			9		6			
7		8				9		5
					2		4	
1					8			
								6

42

		7				5		
			3				4	7
				5				9
		4	6					
	6			4		1	3	
2	1			3				
4	8			9				
9				6				4
		6	2				1	

BONUS!

43

			7	4				
				6			2	4
1								
	9		2					
			9			6		
4		2		1		9	5	
8								1
5		9		7				
	7		6	5				8

44

			1		3			4
5	7				6			9
	4			8	5		6	
2							8	
	9	7						1
							3	
	5				2			
7	2		9					6

45

	9		8	5				7
7		8		4	1		6	
	1		9	6	3			
		4						
6		3			7			8
	3			8			4	6
1					7			
		6						2

46

			1					
		5			7	1	8	4
	8		9	2				
		1			4	6		
		3			5			
							7	
	1	6	4			2		
8						7	9	
7				6				

47

	1							
			9				4	
		9		3	5	8		
7	8		1		3			
		2		6				
6			4		2		3	5
3				1			5	
	6		3	7			8	

48

				7		3		
5	2			4	9			
3						2		
			5					
		2			1		4	8
	9			6				
6						4		
	7							1
				4	9			5

BONUS!

49

	8		2		4			
		9		3				
5				1		8		
	5						1	
	1				5			9
7		3		8				
	7	4			6			
				2		9		3
3				9		5		

50

5	8					4		
	4			2		3		
								7
1				5				9
	6	5						
2			7		6			4
	2	8						5
				4		9		
		1	9				3	

51

				5	3			
	1	8	4		7	5	9	
			6				4	
		7	9				1	
6		2						
				3		8		
	9				1			
	6				9			
		5	8		2			

52

9	4		5					3
		8		7			1	
	3							
				6		2	8	
					9			1
1	7		3			5		
		9	6					
		5	2		4			
			7	3			5	

53

			8		4			
		9		6			3	
		8			1			
		7		5			1	
6			9					
		4		6	5			
5						9		
2		4		9				
	3		5		2		7	

54

		8				6		
		6						4
		3		4		8		
		1		6			4	
	2				1			
			5				9	7
	1		6			5		3
6			7					
7								1

55

								8
			6	7	5	1		
		1				9	6	
	5		4					1
2						7		
	9		5	2		6		
					3	5	9	
	7	5		4				2
		3			9			

56

							6	4
			2			5	9	
3	6	5						1
6		9				8	7	
	1	3						6
							3	
	5	1			8			
4				5	1			
	7				4			

57

4			7					
		3		4				
1				3	2			
6	9							
								3
			9	1	4			8
8	7							9
3				8	6	5		1
			4			8		

58

		2		5				9
	6							
	4				1	5		2
			3		9			
		5		1		2		7
	3	1	6		2			
							9	5
			8	2		7		
9								6

59

							4	1
5				1		6		
			6	2				
4					7	9		
6			5	3	7			4
8								
		4		2		8		7
	1			4	9			3
7			8					

60

				4		5		1
	8				7			
	9	7		2				6
			2			7		
	6				1		4	
1		5			4			9
7								
	3		5					
		6	3				9	

129

1

2	4	9	7	3	6	8	1	5
5	3	7	2	1	8	4	9	6
6	1	8	5	4	9	3	7	2
7	2	1	3	5	4	6	8	9
8	5	4	9	6	2	1	3	7
3	9	6	8	7	1	2	5	4
4	6	3	1	9	7	5	2	8
1	7	2	6	8	5	9	4	3
9	8	5	4	2	3	7	6	1

2

5	9	3	8	1	7	4	2	6
4	7	8	2	6	9	3	1	5
1	6	2	5	4	3	7	8	9
2	3	1	7	9	5	8	6	4
9	4	7	6	3	8	1	5	2
6	8	5	4	2	1	9	7	3
7	1	9	3	5	6	2	4	8
8	2	6	9	7	4	5	3	1
3	5	4	1	8	2	6	9	7

3

6	7	5	1	2	9	4	8	3
3	9	2	8	4	5	6	1	7
4	8	1	3	6	7	5	2	9
7	1	3	5	8	4	2	9	6
5	4	6	9	7	2	1	3	8
8	2	9	6	3	1	7	4	5
9	5	7	4	1	8	3	6	2
1	3	8	2	5	6	9	7	4
2	6	4	7	9	3	8	5	1

4

7	8	9	1	4	5	6	3	2
2	1	4	3	6	9	7	8	5
5	3	6	7	8	2	9	4	1
1	9	2	4	5	6	8	7	3
8	4	7	2	1	3	5	6	9
3	6	5	9	7	8	1	2	4
6	2	3	5	9	7	4	1	8
9	7	1	8	2	4	3	5	6
4	5	8	6	3	1	2	9	7

5

5	6	9	8	1	4	3	7	2
1	7	2	5	3	9	4	6	8
4	8	3	6	7	2	5	9	1
8	9	5	7	6	3	2	1	4
7	2	4	9	8	1	6	3	5
3	1	6	4	2	5	9	8	7
6	5	7	3	4	8	1	2	9
9	3	1	2	5	7	8	4	6
2	4	8	1	9	6	7	5	3

6

1	2	7	5	9	6	3	8	4
4	5	3	7	2	8	6	1	9
9	8	6	4	1	3	7	2	5
3	7	5	1	4	9	8	6	2
6	9	2	8	3	5	4	7	1
8	1	4	6	7	2	9	5	3
5	4	9	2	6	7	1	3	8
7	3	8	9	5	1	2	4	6
2	6	1	3	8	4	5	9	7

7

3	7	8	6	4	9	2	5	1
4	9	1	2	5	7	6	8	3
6	2	5	1	3	8	7	9	4
5	1	7	9	2	3	4	6	8
2	6	3	5	8	4	1	7	9
9	8	4	7	6	1	3	2	5
8	4	2	3	9	6	5	1	7
7	3	6	8	1	5	9	4	2
1	5	9	4	7	2	8	3	6

8

7	6	2	8	1	4	3	5	9
4	9	5	2	3	7	6	8	1
1	8	3	5	6	9	7	2	4
9	4	7	1	8	3	2	6	5
6	3	1	7	2	5	9	4	8
2	5	8	9	4	6	1	3	7
3	1	6	4	9	8	5	7	2
8	7	9	6	5	2	4	1	3
5	2	4	3	7	1	8	9	6

9

8	6	9	4	1	7	3	5	2
4	1	5	2	3	8	7	9	6
3	7	2	6	9	5	1	4	8
9	8	4	1	2	6	5	7	3
7	2	1	8	5	3	4	6	9
6	5	3	7	4	9	2	8	1
5	9	7	3	8	1	6	2	4
1	4	6	9	7	2	8	3	5
2	3	8	5	6	4	9	1	7

10

8	7	3	2	1	4	6	5	9
9	4	1	8	6	5	2	7	3
2	5	6	3	9	7	8	1	4
5	8	7	4	2	3	9	6	1
4	6	2	1	5	9	7	3	8
1	3	9	7	8	6	4	2	5
7	1	8	5	4	2	3	9	6
3	9	5	6	7	8	1	4	2
6	2	4	9	3	1	5	8	7

11

1	8	5	6	4	2	3	9	7
2	9	6	3	5	7	1	4	8
3	4	7	8	1	9	6	5	2
7	3	2	1	9	8	4	6	5
8	5	4	7	6	3	2	1	9
9	6	1	5	2	4	8	7	3
4	2	3	9	7	1	5	8	6
5	1	9	2	8	6	7	3	4
6	7	8	4	3	5	9	2	1

12

1	8	3	4	7	5	9	6	2
9	6	4	3	8	2	5	1	7
7	5	2	9	6	1	8	4	3
3	7	1	2	4	8	6	5	9
8	2	5	6	9	3	1	7	4
4	9	6	1	5	7	3	2	8
5	1	7	8	3	4	2	9	6
2	3	9	7	1	6	4	8	5
6	4	8	5	2	9	7	3	1

13

4	8	9	5	7	1	3	6	2
5	3	2	6	8	9	1	4	7
6	1	7	3	2	4	8	5	9
8	2	1	9	5	7	6	3	4
3	9	6	1	4	8	2	7	5
7	4	5	2	6	3	9	8	1
1	5	8	4	9	6	7	2	3
2	6	3	7	1	5	4	9	8
9	7	4	8	3	2	5	1	6

14

6	4	9	8	7	5	2	3	1
8	7	2	3	4	1	5	9	6
1	3	5	6	9	2	7	4	8
4	5	6	9	1	3	8	7	2
3	1	7	5	2	8	9	6	4
2	9	8	7	6	4	3	1	5
5	6	1	2	3	9	4	8	7
7	2	3	4	8	6	1	5	9
9	8	4	1	5	7	6	2	3

15

8	1	7	9	3	2	5	6	4
9	6	2	4	7	5	1	8	3
4	3	5	1	6	8	9	7	2
6	4	1	2	9	3	7	5	8
5	8	3	7	1	4	6	2	9
7	2	9	8	5	6	3	4	1
2	7	6	3	8	1	4	9	5
1	9	4	5	2	7	8	3	6
3	5	8	6	4	9	2	1	7

16

2	5	6	1	8	7	9	4	3
8	3	9	2	6	4	7	1	5
4	7	1	9	5	3	2	6	8
6	4	5	8	9	1	3	7	2
1	2	7	3	4	5	8	9	6
3	9	8	7	2	6	1	5	4
9	6	3	4	1	2	5	8	7
7	8	4	5	3	9	6	2	1
5	1	2	6	7	8	4	3	9

17

9	6	3	2	7	4	1	8	5
8	2	7	6	5	1	9	4	3
4	5	1	3	8	9	6	7	2
3	8	5	4	6	7	2	1	9
6	7	2	9	1	8	3	5	4
1	9	4	5	2	3	7	6	8
7	3	8	1	4	2	5	9	6
2	1	6	8	9	5	4	3	7
5	4	9	7	3	6	8	2	1

18

4	6	8	7	9	2	3	5	1
9	3	5	8	1	4	2	7	6
2	1	7	5	3	6	9	4	8
7	4	6	3	2	8	5	1	9
1	8	9	4	7	5	6	3	2
3	5	2	1	6	9	7	8	4
5	9	1	6	4	7	8	2	3
8	2	4	9	5	3	1	6	7
6	7	3	2	8	1	4	9	5

19

4	5	1	8	3	9	6	7	2
2	6	7	1	5	4	3	9	8
9	8	3	2	6	7	4	5	1
5	9	6	4	8	3	2	1	7
3	7	4	5	1	2	9	8	6
8	1	2	7	9	6	5	3	4
6	4	8	9	7	5	1	2	3
1	2	9	3	4	8	7	6	5
7	3	5	6	2	1	8	4	9

20

3	4	5	9	8	6	1	7	2
6	7	1	2	3	4	8	5	9
9	2	8	5	1	7	6	3	4
5	9	4	1	2	3	7	8	6
2	3	7	8	6	9	5	4	1
8	1	6	7	4	5	2	9	3
1	8	9	3	7	2	4	6	5
4	5	2	6	9	8	3	1	7
7	6	3	4	5	1	9	2	8

21

5	8	2	1	6	9	4	3	7
7	6	4	2	3	5	1	9	8
9	3	1	8	7	4	2	6	5
2	5	3	4	9	1	8	7	6
1	7	8	6	5	3	9	4	2
4	9	6	7	8	2	3	5	1
3	1	7	9	2	6	5	8	4
8	4	9	5	1	7	6	2	3
6	2	5	3	4	8	7	1	9

22

7	5	3	2	8	1	6	9	4
8	2	4	3	9	6	1	5	7
6	9	1	7	5	4	3	2	8
5	8	2	1	4	3	7	6	9
1	7	9	8	6	5	2	4	3
3	4	6	9	7	2	8	1	5
2	1	8	4	3	9	5	7	6
9	3	5	6	2	7	4	8	1
4	6	7	5	1	8	9	3	2

23

1	9	7	6	3	5	4	8	2
5	3	2	4	9	8	1	7	6
8	4	6	7	1	2	3	5	9
4	7	9	2	6	1	5	3	8
3	1	8	5	4	9	6	2	7
6	2	5	8	7	3	9	4	1
9	8	1	3	2	4	7	6	5
2	6	3	9	5	7	8	1	4
7	5	4	1	8	6	2	9	3

24

1	9	2	4	8	6	3	7	5
6	4	8	5	3	7	1	2	9
7	3	5	1	2	9	8	6	4
3	2	7	8	9	5	4	1	6
4	5	6	2	1	3	7	9	8
8	1	9	6	7	4	2	5	3
5	6	3	7	4	2	9	8	1
2	8	4	9	6	1	5	3	7
9	7	1	3	5	8	6	4	2

25

9	2	5	3	1	6	8	7	4
8	4	3	9	2	7	5	6	1
1	7	6	5	8	4	2	3	9
5	9	2	8	7	1	6	4	3
7	3	1	4	6	5	9	8	2
6	8	4	2	3	9	7	1	5
3	1	9	7	5	8	4	2	6
4	6	8	1	9	2	3	5	7
2	5	7	6	4	3	1	9	8

26

2	4	9	5	6	8	3	7	1
6	7	1	3	2	4	9	8	5
8	3	5	9	1	7	2	4	6
3	5	2	4	8	9	6	1	7
4	9	6	7	5	1	8	3	2
7	1	8	2	3	6	4	5	9
1	6	3	8	9	5	7	2	4
5	8	4	6	7	2	1	9	3
9	2	7	1	4	3	5	6	8

27

7	6	2	8	5	3	1	9	4
4	5	8	2	9	1	3	7	6
3	9	1	4	7	6	5	2	8
9	2	4	7	3	8	6	5	1
5	7	6	9	1	4	8	3	2
1	8	3	5	6	2	9	4	7
8	3	7	1	4	9	2	6	5
6	1	5	3	2	7	4	8	9
2	4	9	6	8	5	7	1	3

28

8	6	1	4	5	3	2	7	9
2	9	5	8	1	7	4	6	3
7	4	3	6	9	2	5	8	1
9	8	6	2	4	1	7	3	5
4	3	2	5	7	8	1	9	6
1	5	7	3	6	9	8	2	4
3	2	9	1	8	4	6	5	7
5	7	4	9	2	6	3	1	8
6	1	8	7	3	5	9	4	2

29

6	3	1	7	9	8	5	2	4
8	2	5	6	3	4	1	7	9
4	7	9	1	2	5	8	6	3
2	4	7	8	6	1	9	3	5
5	1	3	9	4	2	6	8	7
9	8	6	3	5	7	4	1	2
3	9	8	4	7	6	2	5	1
1	5	4	2	8	3	7	9	6
7	6	2	5	1	9	3	4	8

30

8	5	1	6	2	9	7	3	4
7	9	4	5	1	3	8	6	2
2	6	3	8	4	7	5	1	9
1	7	5	2	9	6	3	4	8
4	8	9	1	3	5	6	2	7
3	2	6	4	7	8	1	9	5
6	3	7	9	5	2	4	8	1
5	1	2	3	8	4	9	7	6
9	4	8	7	6	1	2	5	3

31

7	8	2	9	4	6	5	3	1
6	3	9	1	5	8	7	2	4
5	4	1	7	2	3	8	9	6
3	9	7	2	6	4	1	5	8
8	1	4	5	9	7	3	6	2
2	5	6	3	8	1	9	4	7
9	7	5	6	1	2	4	8	3
1	2	8	4	3	5	6	7	9
4	6	3	8	7	9	2	1	5

32

5	8	6	4	3	2	1	9	7
4	7	1	6	8	9	5	2	3
9	3	2	7	1	5	8	4	6
6	9	3	1	7	8	2	5	4
7	1	5	2	4	3	6	8	9
2	4	8	9	5	6	3	7	1
8	6	9	3	2	7	4	1	5
1	5	7	8	6	4	9	3	2
3	2	4	5	9	1	7	6	8

33

2	7	6	5	3	1	8	9	4
5	3	1	8	9	4	2	7	6
9	8	4	6	7	2	1	5	3
4	2	8	7	5	3	6	1	9
7	9	5	4	1	6	3	8	2
6	1	3	2	8	9	7	4	5
3	5	9	1	2	7	4	6	8
8	6	7	3	4	5	9	2	1
1	4	2	9	6	8	5	3	7

34

9	8	5	3	2	6	1	4	7
3	7	1	5	4	8	9	2	6
4	6	2	9	1	7	8	3	5
5	2	8	1	7	3	6	9	4
7	9	4	6	8	2	5	1	3
6	1	3	4	9	5	7	8	2
2	4	7	8	5	1	3	6	9
8	3	9	7	6	4	2	5	1
1	5	6	2	3	9	4	7	8

35

6	4	2	3	9	8	5	7	1
8	7	9	5	4	1	6	2	3
5	3	1	2	6	7	4	9	8
1	8	4	7	3	2	9	5	6
9	5	3	6	1	4	7	8	2
7	2	6	8	5	9	1	3	4
3	6	7	4	2	5	8	1	9
4	1	5	9	8	3	2	6	7
2	9	8	1	7	6	3	4	5

36

3	7	6	9	5	1	2	4	8
4	1	2	7	3	8	6	9	5
5	9	8	6	2	4	1	7	3
9	6	7	2	4	5	8	3	1
2	8	4	3	1	6	9	5	7
1	5	3	8	9	7	4	2	6
6	3	1	4	7	9	5	8	2
7	4	5	1	8	2	3	6	9
8	2	9	5	6	3	7	1	4

37

8	7	2	5	1	3	4	6	9
9	3	1	4	6	7	8	5	2
6	5	4	8	2	9	1	3	7
1	6	8	2	7	4	3	9	5
7	2	9	1	3	5	6	4	8
3	4	5	9	8	6	2	7	1
5	1	6	3	9	8	7	2	4
4	8	7	6	5	2	9	1	3
2	9	3	7	4	1	5	8	6

38

9	1	2	5	7	4	8	3	6
3	7	6	9	1	8	5	4	2
4	5	8	3	2	6	9	7	1
2	3	7	1	8	5	4	6	9
1	6	9	2	4	3	7	8	5
5	8	4	7	6	9	1	2	3
7	2	3	4	5	1	6	9	8
8	4	5	6	9	2	3	1	7
6	9	1	8	3	7	2	5	4

39

1	9	7	2	8	3	5	4	6
6	2	8	9	5	4	7	1	3
5	4	3	7	6	1	9	8	2
8	5	2	1	7	6	3	9	4
7	3	4	8	9	2	6	5	1
9	1	6	4	3	5	2	7	8
2	7	9	6	4	8	1	3	5
4	6	5	3	1	9	8	2	7
3	8	1	5	2	7	4	6	9

40

6	1	4	2	9	5	3	8	7
7	2	3	8	4	1	9	6	5
5	8	9	3	6	7	4	2	1
4	6	1	9	5	8	7	3	2
8	5	7	1	2	3	6	9	4
9	3	2	4	7	6	1	5	8
3	9	5	7	8	4	2	1	6
1	7	8	6	3	2	5	4	9
2	4	6	5	1	9	8	7	3

41

6	7	3	9	2	5	1	8	4
8	2	4	7	1	3	5	6	9
9	5	1	6	8	4	7	2	3
2	1	9	5	3	6	4	7	8
3	4	5	8	9	7	6	1	2
7	6	8	2	4	1	9	3	5
5	9	7	3	6	2	8	4	1
1	3	6	4	5	8	2	9	7
4	8	2	1	7	9	3	5	6

42

3	9	7	4	2	8	5	6	1
6	5	2	3	1	9	8	4	7
1	4	8	7	5	6	3	2	9
8	3	4	6	7	1	2	9	5
7	6	5	9	4	2	1	3	8
2	1	9	8	3	5	4	7	6
4	8	3	1	9	7	6	5	2
9	2	1	5	6	3	7	8	4
5	7	6	2	8	4	9	1	3

43

6	2	8	7	4	9	1	3	5
9	5	3	1	8	6	7	2	4
1	4	7	5	2	3	6	8	9
3	9	5	2	6	4	8	1	7
7	8	1	9	3	5	4	6	2
4	6	2	8	1	7	9	5	3
8	3	6	4	9	2	5	7	1
5	1	9	3	7	8	2	4	6
2	7	4	6	5	1	3	9	8

44

9	8	2	1	5	3	6	7	4
5	7	4	8	2	6	3	1	9
1	3	6	4	9	7	8	2	5
3	4	1	2	8	5	9	6	7
2	6	5	7	1	9	4	8	3
8	9	7	3	6	4	2	5	1
6	1	9	5	4	8	7	3	2
4	5	3	6	7	2	1	9	8
7	2	8	9	3	1	5	4	6

45

3	9	1	8	5	6	4	2	7
4	6	2	3	7	9	8	5	1
7	5	8	2	4	1	3	6	9
8	1	5	9	6	3	2	7	4
9	7	4	5	2	8	6	1	3
6	2	3	4	1	7	5	9	8
2	3	7	1	8	5	9	4	6
1	4	9	6	3	2	7	8	5
5	8	6	7	9	4	1	3	2

46

3	6	7	1	4	8	9	2	5
2	9	5	6	3	7	1	8	4
1	8	4	9	2	5	3	6	7
5	2	1	7	8	4	6	3	9
6	7	8	3	1	9	5	4	2
4	3	9	5	6	2	8	7	1
9	1	6	4	7	3	2	5	8
8	4	3	2	5	1	7	9	6
7	5	2	8	9	6	4	1	3

47

2	1	6	8	4	7	5	9	3
8	5	3	9	2	1	6	4	7
4	7	9	6	3	5	8	2	1
7	8	4	1	5	3	2	6	9
5	3	2	7	6	9	4	1	8
6	9	1	4	8	2	7	3	5
3	4	7	2	1	8	9	5	6
1	2	8	5	9	6	3	7	4
9	6	5	3	7	4	1	8	2

48

8	1	4	9	2	7	5	3	6
5	2	6	1	3	4	9	8	7
3	7	9	8	5	6	1	2	4
4	6	3	5	7	8	2	1	9
7	5	2	3	9	1	6	4	8
1	9	8	4	6	2	7	5	3
6	8	5	7	1	3	4	9	2
9	4	7	2	8	5	3	6	1
2	3	1	6	4	9	8	7	5

49

6	8	1	2	7	4	3	9	5
2	4	9	5	3	8	6	7	1
5	3	7	6	1	9	8	2	4
4	5	2	9	6	3	7	1	8
8	1	6	7	4	5	2	3	9
7	9	3	1	8	2	4	5	6
9	7	4	3	5	6	1	8	2
1	6	5	8	2	7	9	4	3
3	2	8	4	9	1	5	6	7

50

5	8	6	3	9	7	4	1	2
7	4	9	1	2	5	3	6	8
3	1	2	4	6	8	9	5	7
1	7	4	8	5	3	6	2	9
8	6	5	2	4	9	1	7	3
2	9	3	7	1	6	5	8	4
9	2	8	6	3	1	7	4	5
6	3	7	5	8	4	2	9	1
4	5	1	9	7	2	8	3	6

51

7	4	6	8	9	5	3	2	1
3	1	8	4	2	7	5	9	6
5	2	9	6	3	1	8	4	7
4	8	7	9	5	2	6	1	3
6	3	2	1	4	8	7	5	9
9	5	1	7	6	3	4	8	2
8	9	4	2	7	6	1	3	5
2	6	5	3	1	4	9	7	8
1	7	3	5	8	9	2	6	4

52

9	4	7	5	1	6	8	2	3
2	5	8	9	7	3	4	1	6
6	3	1	8	4	2	7	9	5
5	9	3	1	6	7	2	8	4
8	6	2	4	5	9	3	7	1
1	7	4	3	2	8	5	6	9
3	2	9	6	8	5	1	4	7
7	1	5	2	9	4	6	3	8
4	8	6	7	3	1	9	5	2

53

1	6	3	7	8	9	4	2	5
4	2	9	1	6	5	7	3	8
7	5	8	3	2	4	1	6	9
8	4	7	2	5	3	9	1	6
6	1	5	9	7	8	3	4	2
3	9	2	4	1	6	5	8	7
5	8	1	6	3	7	2	9	4
2	7	4	8	9	1	6	5	3
9	3	6	5	4	2	8	7	1

54

9	4	8	1	3	5	7	6	2
1	5	6	8	7	2	9	3	4
2	7	3	9	4	6	8	1	5
5	9	1	3	6	7	2	4	8
8	2	7	4	9	1	3	5	6
3	6	4	5	2	8	1	9	7
4	1	2	6	8	9	5	7	3
6	8	5	7	1	3	4	2	9
7	3	9	2	5	4	6	8	1

55

5	6	4	9	1	2	3	7	8
8	3	9	6	7	5	1	2	4
7	2	1	8	3	4	9	6	5
3	5	6	4	9	7	2	8	1
2	4	8	3	6	1	7	5	9
1	9	7	5	2	8	6	4	3
4	1	2	7	8	3	5	9	6
9	7	5	1	4	6	8	3	2
6	8	3	2	5	9	4	1	7

56

2	9	7	1	8	5	3	6	4
1	8	4	2	3	6	5	9	7
3	6	5	4	7	9	2	8	1
6	4	9	5	1	3	8	7	2
7	1	3	8	9	2	4	5	6
5	2	8	6	4	7	1	3	9
9	5	1	7	2	8	6	4	3
4	3	6	9	5	1	7	2	8
8	7	2	3	6	4	9	1	5

57

4	2	8	9	7	6	1	3	5
9	5	3	2	1	4	8	7	6
1	6	7	5	8	3	2	9	4
6	9	4	8	3	2	5	1	7
2	8	1	4	5	7	9	6	3
7	3	5	6	9	1	4	2	8
8	7	2	1	6	5	3	4	9
3	4	9	7	2	8	6	5	1
5	1	6	3	4	9	7	8	2

58

1	7	2	3	8	5	6	4	9
5	6	9	2	7	4	1	8	3
8	4	3	9	6	1	5	7	2
4	2	8	5	3	7	9	6	1
6	9	5	4	1	8	2	3	7
7	3	1	6	9	2	4	5	8
2	8	7	1	4	6	3	9	5
3	5	6	8	2	9	7	1	4
9	1	4	7	5	3	8	2	6

59

9	6	7	2	5	8	3	4	1
5	4	2	3	7	1	9	6	8
1	8	3	4	9	6	2	7	5
4	3	5	1	8	2	7	9	6
6	2	9	5	3	7	1	8	4
8	7	1	9	6	4	5	3	2
3	9	4	6	2	5	8	1	7
2	1	8	7	4	9	6	5	3
7	5	6	8	1	3	4	2	9

60

6	2	3	9	4	8	5	7	1
4	8	1	6	5	7	9	3	2
5	9	7	1	2	3	4	8	6
3	4	9	2	6	5	7	1	8
2	6	8	7	9	1	3	4	5
1	7	5	8	3	4	2	6	9
7	1	2	4	8	9	6	5	3
9	3	4	5	1	6	8	2	7
8	5	6	3	7	2	1	9	4

Printed in Great Britain
by Amazon